180 DAYS of Math
for Eighth Grade

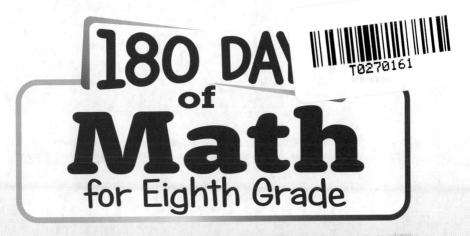

Author

Darlene Misconish Tyler, M.A.Ed.

Consultant

Angela Gallo, M.A.Ed.
Richardson Independent School District

Program Credits

Corinne Burton, M.A.Ed., *President and Publisher*
Emily R. Smith, M.A.Ed., *SVP of Content Development*
Véronique Bos, *VP of Creative*
Lynette Ordoñez, *Content Manager*
Melissa Laughlin, *Editor*
Avery Rabedeaux, *Assistant Editor*
Jill Malcolm, *Graphic Designer*

Image Credits: all images from Shutterstock and/or iStock

Standards

© Copyright 2010 National Governors Association Center for Best Practices and Council of Chief State School Officers. All rights reserved.
© Copyright 2007–2024 Texas Education Agency (TEA). All Rights Reserved.
© 2024 TESOL International Association
© 2024 Board of Regents of the University of Wisconsin System

A division of Teacher Created Materials
5482 Argosy Avenue
Huntington Beach, CA 92649
www.tcmpub.com/shell-education
ISBN 979-8-7659-5279-5
© 2025 Shell Educational Publishing, Inc.
Printed by: 51497
Printed in: China

Table of Contents

Introduction

180 Days of Practice

Appendix

Math Education Today

As many adults can attest, whether they are teaching in a classroom or supporting children learning math at home, mathematics does not seem to be the same as how they learned it growing up. Instruction today focuses on critical thinking, problem solving, and using a variety of strategies to find answers. Current mathematics instruction might look different, but math still focuses on helping students become skillful problem solvers. Students are encouraged to think like mathematicians. Mathematics instruction seeks to build students' mathematical reasoning skills and to ensure students can apply concepts to real-world problems.

Prior to the 1990s, individual states created their own standards for student learning. This created a disparity in achievement among graduating high school seniors. To help make student education more consistent across the country, the National Governor's Association and the Council of Chief State School Offices set out to develop national standards with the intent of improving student learning and achievement (Marchitello and Wilhelm 2014). Over time, these standards were honed, improved, and updated using cognitive science and research regarding children's learning.

That research became a cornerstone in the philosophy of current math education—making sure students have a conceptual understanding of something before moving to the more abstract ways to solve problems. In the past, students might have learned only one way to solve a math problem. Research from Vanderbilt University shows it is more beneficial to introduce students to more than one problem-solving strategy (Durkin, Rittle-Johnson, and Star 2017). Knowing multiple strategies allows students to better understand a concept and helps them find efficient approaches that make the best sense to them.

Though mathematics education may look different today, the solutions to mathematical problems remain the same. Students today are taking time to think deeply, reason abstractly, and understand numbers in ways that will prepare them to be successful in college and their careers.

Refining Math Skills

Children learn math best when they can see, organize, and interpret through tools or models. Learning begins with concrete representations of mathematical concepts (Cathcart et al. 2014). Manipulatives, such as counters, base-ten blocks, and coins, are effective tools for students to use to build concrete representations. Students can then progress to drawing pictorial models of concrete objects, such as tallies, circles, and dots. These steps prepare students to learn the abstract qualities of mathematical concepts, making connections between the objects, pictures, and equations or formulas.

Problem-solving is the context in which students can extend current understanding to new situations and make connections between mathematical ideas and the real world. Rote practice in mathematics limits students' creativity and hinders their ability to problem solve and apply math in real-life situations. Problems are easier to solve when students can draw upon their practical, real-world knowledge (McNeil and Jarvin 2007).

Math Education Today *(cont.)*

Building Math Fluency

There is an emphasis on national mathematics standards for students to be able to solve math problems accurately and efficiently. While this mathematical fluency is certainly expected, it is important to realize that conceptual understanding is the basis for developing fluency. When a student understands combinations of tens, developed through many experiences using a ten frame, they can extend that understanding to learn more difficult addition facts. For example, a student can think

about $9 + 6$ as taking 1 from the 6 and adding it to the 9, so the fact now becomes $10 + 5$, which equals 15. To assess students' fluency, evaluate their flexibility, accuracy, efficiency, and appropriate strategy use when solving math problems.

Learning math is not a "one and done" achievement. A spiral curriculum model was introduced by psychologist Jerome Bruner in 1960, and continuing research agrees that it greatly benefits students (Ireland and Mouthaan 2020). A spiral approach means concepts are spread out over time and reviewed frequently. When students have repeated exposure to a skill, they are more likely to understand and remember it.

Research to Practice

180 Days of Math incorporates a balanced approach to develop both conceptual understanding and mathematical fluency.

- Practice pages encourage students to find and use manipulatives, such as those provided in the digital resources, when solving problems.
- Instructional pages and practice pages provide students numerous opportunities to learn concepts through visual models and showcase their understanding by drawing their own pictorial representations.
- A variety of rich math tasks, or word problems, allow students to apply mathematical concepts and operations to real-world situations.
- Instructional pages and sidebars on practice pages model a variety of strategies to help students build proficiency.
- Five-day spiral reviews at the end of each unit touch on concepts taught throughout the entire book up to that point, not just the current unit.

How to Use This Resource

Instructional Pages

The math concepts in this resource are organized into five units. Each unit is divided into sections that focus on specific standards-based topics. To introduce mathematical concepts, there are instructional pages at the beginnings of the sections. These pages support students so they can complete the practice pages with confidence and accuracy.

An overview of big ideas, important concepts, and key vocabulary essential to the upcoming pages is explained in grade-appropriate language.

Example problems model problem-solving steps and strategies that students can follow.

Students answer guiding questions, attempt the modeled strategies, and solve problems with support.

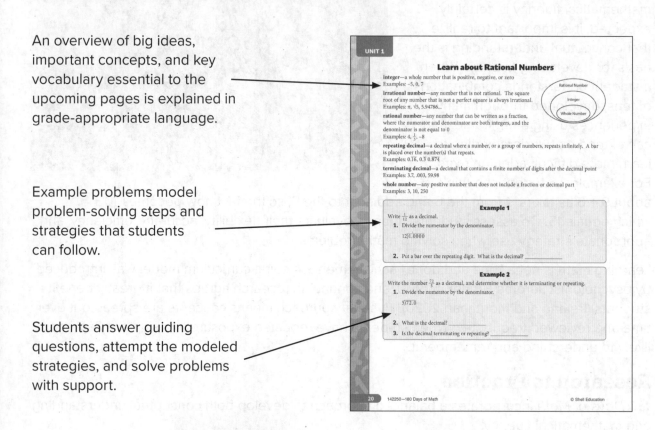

How to Use This Resource *(cont.)*

Practice Pages

Practice pages are provided for every day of the school year to reinforce grade-level concepts and skills. The practice pages can be easily prepared and implemented as part of a morning routine, at the beginning of each math lesson, or as homework. Each day's math skills are aligned to state mathematics standards. (A chart with these standards can be found on pages 220–221.)

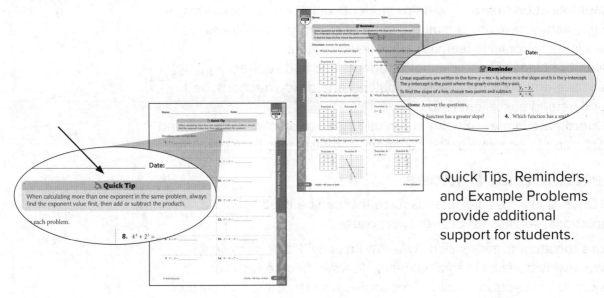

Quick Tips, Reminders, and Example Problems provide additional support for students.

Review Pages

Review is embedded throughout this resource to support students' retention of mathematical concepts.

The first section of practice pages in this resource reviews the math concepts from the previous grade. This activates students' prior knowledge after summer break and offers teachers and families a quick view of students' grade-level readiness.

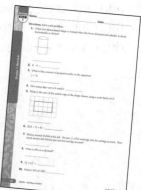

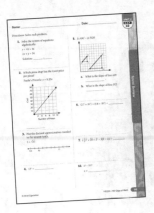

Spiral review pages at the end of each unit include additional practice in the concepts learned. This helps ensure that students' skills and content knowledge remain fresh, and it helps them build fluency as the year goes on.

A cumulative review serves as the last section of practice pages in this resource, allowing students to showcase their understanding of all grade-level math concepts practiced throughout the year.

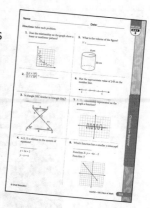

How to Use This Resource *(cont.)*

Digital Math Learning Resources

A variety of math resources are provided digitally (see page 240 for instructions on how to download these pages). These quick references and tools support students in understanding and solving many different problem types. You may choose to print the resources ahead of time or as needed. Some of the resources available include the following:

- **Multiplication Chart**—This helps students quickly reference math facts if they have not committed them to memory. This allows students to continue learning grade-level content.
- **Number Lines**—These can help students add and subtract positive and negative numbers, multiply and divide fractions, and understand equivalent ratios.
- **Coordinate Planes**—Students can use these to practice with ordered pairs and to better visualize equations and distances between points.

Instructional Options

180 Days of Math is a flexible resource that can be used in various instructional settings for different purposes.

- Use the student pages as daily warm-up activities or as review.
- Work with students in small groups, allowing them to focus on specific concepts and skills. This setting also lends itself to partner and group discussions about problem-solving strategies.
- Student pages in this resource can be completed independently during center times and as activities for early finishers.

How to Use This Resource *(cont.)*

Diagnostic Assessment

The practice pages in this book can be used as diagnostic assessments. These activity pages require students to think critically, use problem-solving strategies, and utilize mathematical skills and content knowledge. (An answer key is provided starting on page 223.)

The diagnostic analysis tools included in the digital resources allow for quick evaluation and ongoing monitoring of student work. See at a glance which math topics students may need to focus on further to develop proficiency.

Analysis sheets are provided as *Microsoft Word®* files in the digital resources. There is a *Class Analysis Sheet* and an *Individual Analysis Sheet*. Use the file that matches your assessment needs. After each review section, record how many answers each student got correct on the analysis sheet. Then, analyze the data on the analysis sheet to determine instructional needs for your child or class.

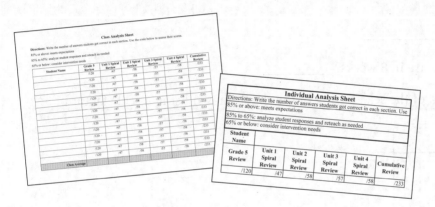

Using the Results to Differentiate Instruction

Once results are gathered and analyzed, use the data to inform differentiation. The data can help determine which concepts are the most difficult for students and which students need additional instructional support and continued practice. The results of the diagnostic analysis may show that the class is struggling with a particular topic.

The results of the diagnostic analysis may also show that an individual or small group of students is struggling with a particular concept or group of concepts. Consider pulling aside these students while others are working independently to instruct further on the concept(s). You can also use the results to help identify individuals or groups of proficient students who are ready for enrichment or above-grade-level instruction. These students may benefit from independent learning contracts or more challenging activities.

Name: _____ Date: _____

Grade 7 Review

Directions: Solve each problem.

1. What two-dimensional shape is formed when the three-dimensional cylinder is sliced horizontally, as shown?

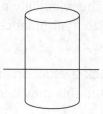

_____

2. $4^2 \cdot 4^3 =$ _____

3. What is the constant of proportionality in the equation?

$y = 5x$

_____

4. How many days are in 8 weeks? _____

5. What is the area of the scaled copy of the shape shown using a scale factor of 3?

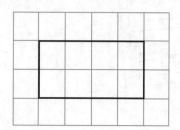

_____

6. $2[3(5 - 7) + 4] =$ _____

7. Mickey earned \$2,000 at his job. He put $\frac{3}{5}$ of his earnings into his savings account. How much money did Mickey put into his savings account?

_____

8. What is 40% as a decimal?

_____

9. $3\frac{1}{5} + 5\frac{2}{7} =$ _____

10. What is 35% of 300? _____

Name: _____ **Date:** _____

Directions: Solve each problem.

1. Is the relationship shown on the graph proportional?

   _____

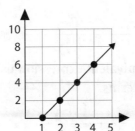

2. $9\frac{3}{4} - 7\frac{1}{3} =$ _____

3. Write an addition equation to represent the diagram.

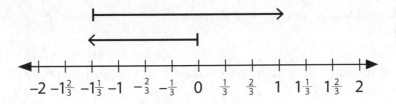

   _____

4. Write $\frac{2}{3}$ as a decimal. _____

5. What is the constant of proportionality shown in the table? _____

x	y
6	30
8	40
10	50

6. Write an expression for *twice a number increased by eleven*.

   _____

7. $5x - 7 > 38$

   $x >$ _____

8. Graph your answer to problem 7 on the number line.

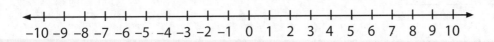

9. $(3^2)^3 =$ _____

10. $-80 \div (-4) =$ _____

Grade 7 Review

Name: _____ **Date:** _____

Directions: Solve each problem.

1. $10\frac{7}{8} - 4\frac{3}{5} =$ _____

2. Write an equivalent expression using the Distributive Property. Then, label the diagram with the correct terms.

   $5a + 25 =$ _____

   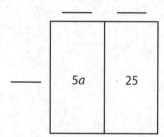

3. Kim read 120 pages in $\frac{2}{3}$ of an hour. How many pages could Kim read in 1 hour?

   _____

4. $9\frac{3}{8} \times 8 =$ _____

5. A recipe calls for $2\frac{1}{2}$ cups of sugar. Myron has 14 cups of sugar. How many batches can Myron make?

   _____

6. Write a subtraction equation to find the difference between the integers on the number line, and then solve the equation.

   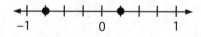

   _____

7. Reese earned $435 for 30 hours of work. How much did Reese earn per hour?

   _____

8. Find the missing side length.

   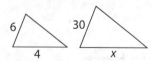

   $x =$ _____

9. Mateo purchased 2 boxes of golf balls for $71. How much would Mateo pay if he purchased 7 boxes?

   _____

10. How many minutes are in 11 days? _____

Name: _____   Date: _____

Directions: Solve each problem.

1. How many triangles can be drawn with angles of 50°, 50°, and 90°?

_____

2. Graph the proportional relationship.

$y = 1x$

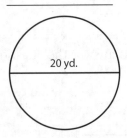

3. What is the circumference of the circle?

_____

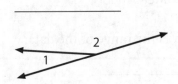

20 yd.

4. What kind of angles are angles 1 and 2?

_____

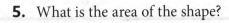

5. What is the area of the shape?

_____

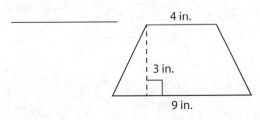

4 in.

3 in.

9 in.

6. Write an equation to represent the relationship on the graph.

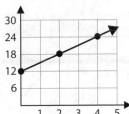

$y =$ _____

7. $-64 \div 8 =$ _____

8. $4^4 \cdot 4^2 =$ _____

9. Heidi wants to leave a 20% tip on her bill of $45. How much money should she leave, including the tip?

_____

10. If a circle has a circumference of 64π units, what is the diameter?

_____

Name: _____   **Date:** _____

Directions: Solve each problem.

1. What is the measure of the missing angle?

_____

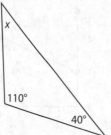

2. What is the constant of proportionality represented on the graph?

_____

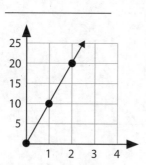

3. Use the figures to solve for x.

$x =$ _____

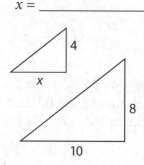

4. Find the area of the figure.

$A =$ _____

5. Write and solve an equation to find the missing angle.

_____

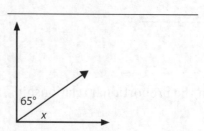

6. Write an equivalent expression using the Distributive Property. Use the diagram to help.

$7(2x + 3y + 8) =$ _____

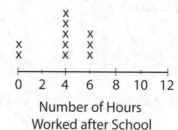

7. Use the line plot to answer the questions.

```
        x
        x
        x    x
  x     x    x
  x     x    x
  +--+--+--+--+--+--+
  0  2  4  6  8  10 12
      Number of Hours
    Worked after School
```

a. What is the range of the data?

_____

b. What is the median number of hours worked after school?

_____

8. $3\frac{1}{2} \times 1\frac{1}{3} =$ _____

Directions: Solve each problem.

1. What type of angles are angles 1 and 2?

_____

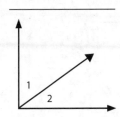

2. What is the area of the triangle?

A = _____

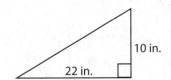

10 in.

22 in.

3. Find the area of the figure.

A = _____

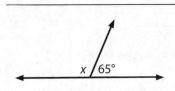

6

3

5

2

2

4. Write and solve an equation to find the missing angle measure.

_____

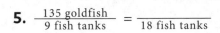

x / 65°

5. $\dfrac{135 \text{ goldfish}}{9 \text{ fish tanks}} = \dfrac{\underline{\quad\quad}}{18 \text{ fish tanks}}$

6. Janine baked 14 pies in 7 days. If she baked the same number of pies each day, how many pies did Janine bake in 1 day?

_____

7. Is the relationship shown in the table proportional? _____

x	y
9	36
10	40
11	55

8. The area of a circle is 121π square units. What is the radius of the circle?

_____

9. Marjorie read 40 books in 8 days. If she read the same number of books each day, how many books did she read in 4 days?

_____

10. $-55 \div (-11) =$ _____

Name: _____ Date: _____

Directions: Solve each problem.

1. Find the area as a decimal approximation.

_____

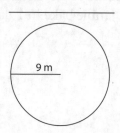

9 m

2. Write and solve an equation to find the missing angle measure.

_____

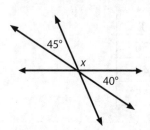

45°

x

40°

3. The football coach ordered 50 new helmets for $3,000. How much would 30 helmets cost?

_____

4. $5^3 + 2^2 =$ _____

5. What is the constant of proportionality in the given equation?

$y = 0.5x$

_____

6. Write an equation for the proportional relationship: Li has 140 stamps in 4 books.

$y =$ _____

7. $3(9 - 11) + 5 - (-6) + 3^2 =$ _____

8. Complete the table.

Fraction	Decimal	Percent
$\frac{3}{4}$		
	0.32	
		15%

9. There were 24 people equally grouped in 6 cars. How many people were in each car?

_____

10. $\frac{15}{x} = \frac{90}{60}$

$x =$ _____

142250—180 Days of Math

Directions: Solve each problem.

1. What is the area of the parallelogram?

A = _____

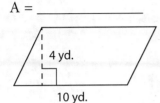

4 yd.

10 yd.

2. Write an equation to represent the proportional relationship on the graph.

$y =$ _____

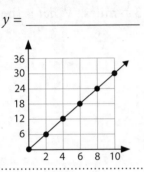

3. What is the volume of the prism?

_____

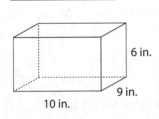

6 in.

9 in.

10 in.

4. Pierre and his friends ate at a restaurant. The bill was $92, but they wanted to leave a 15% tip. How much did they pay, including the tip?

_____

5. What is the circumference of the circle in terms of pi?

_____

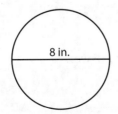

8 in.

6. Can a triangle be formed with side lengths of 8 cm, 10 cm, and 15 cm?

_____

7. $4(3 - 6) - (8 - 7) + 5^2 =$ _____

8. Hank is buying a new pair of boots for $130. There is a tax of 8% on the boots. What is the total cost of the boots, including tax?

_____

9. $40 - (-9) =$ _____

10. $8 (-3) =$ _____

Name: _____ **Date:** _____

Directions: Solve each problem.

1. Is the relationship shown on the graph proportional? _____

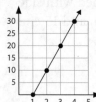

2. How many hours are in 2 weeks? _____

3. Write $\frac{3}{8}$ as a decimal. _____

4. Polly walked $6\frac{3}{4}$ miles. Rami walked 7.04 miles. Megan walked $3\frac{1}{5}$ miles. What is the total number of miles they walked? _____

5. Write and solve an equation to find the missing angle measure.

_____

6. Milo drove 1,904 miles in 34 hours at a constant speed. How many miles did Milo drive each hour? _____

7. Taryn is doing homework for 80 minutes. She spent $\frac{1}{8}$ of the 80 minutes on her Spanish homework. How many minutes did Taryn spend on her Spanish homework?

_____

8. $4\frac{1}{4} + \frac{7}{8} - (-2) =$ _____

9. Simplify the expression.

$15m - 3n + 8n - 6 - 9m$

_____

10. Is 2 a solution to the given equation? Circle your answer.

$8(2x + 5) = 40$

yes   no

Directions: Solve each problem.

1. Write the circumference of the circle as a decimal approximation.

   _____

   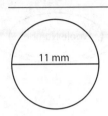

   11 mm

2. Write an equation to represent the proportional relationship shown on the graph.

   $y =$ _____

   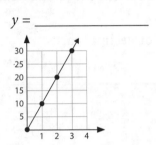

3. What is the area of the figure?

   A = _____

   8

   2

   7

   5

   4

4. What is the constant of proportionality shown in the table? $k =$ _____

x	y
0	0
4	32
8	64
12	96

5. What is the circumference of a circle with a diameter of 5 in terms of pi?

   _____

6. Gil saved $300 over 10 months. At that rate, how much money could Gil save over 12 months?

   _____

7. Miko bought 3.85 pints of strawberries and $5\frac{1}{4}$ pints of raspberries. How many total pints of berries did Miko buy?

   _____

8. The walk to the park is 9 miles. Jermaine walked $\frac{2}{3}$ of the way to the park. How many miles did Jermaine walk?

   _____

9. $-7 + (-11) =$ _____

10. Can a triangle have side lengths of 4 inches, 7 inches, and 11 inches?

    _____

Learn about Rational Numbers

integer—a whole number that is positive, negative, or 0
Examples: –5, 0, 7

irrational number—any number that is not rational. The square root of any number that is not a perfect square is always irrational.
Examples: π, $\sqrt{5}$, 5.94786...

rational number—any number that can be written as a fraction, where the numerator and denominator are both integers, and the denominator is not equal to 0
Examples: 4, $\frac{1}{3}$, –8

repeating decimal—a decimal where a number, or a group of numbers, repeats infinitely. A bar is placed over the number(s) that repeats.
Examples: $0.\overline{16}$, $0.\overline{3}$ $0.\overline{874}$

terminating decimal—a decimal that contains a finite number of digits after the decimal point
Examples: 3.7, .003, 59.98

whole number—any positive number that does not include a fraction or decimal part
Examples: 3, 10, 250

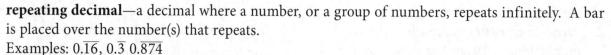

Example 1

Write $\frac{1}{12}$ as a decimal.

1. Divide the numerator by the denominator.

$$12\overline{)1.0000}$$

2. Put a bar over the repeating digit. What is the decimal? _____

Example 2

Write the number $\frac{72}{5}$ as a decimal, and determine whether it is terminating or repeating.

1. Divide the numerator by the denominator.

$$5\overline{)72.0}$$

2. What is the decimal? _____

3. Is the decimal terminating or repeating? _____

Learn about Rational Numbers *(cont.)*

Example 3

Write the repeating decimal as a fraction.

$0.\overline{15}$

1. Let $x = 0.151515\ldots$

2. Multiply both sides of the equation by a power of 10 equal to the number of digits that repeat. There are 2 repeating digits, so multiply by 10^2, or 100. (If there were only one repeating digit, you would multiply by 10.)

   $100x = 15.151515\ldots$

3. Subtract $x = 0.151515\ldots$ from the equation.

$$\begin{array}{r} 100x = 15.151515\ldots \\ -\quad x = -0.151515\ldots \\ \hline 99x = 15 \end{array}$$

4. Divide both sides of the equation by 99.

   $\dfrac{99x}{99} = \dfrac{15}{99}$

   $x = \dfrac{15}{99}$ or $\dfrac{5}{33}$

5. Check your answer. If you divide your numerator by your denominator, you should get $0.151515\ldots$

Example 4

Write the number as an improper fraction.

1.4

1. What decimal place is the 4 located in? _____

2. 0.4 as a fraction is $\dfrac{4}{10}$ or $\dfrac{2}{5}$.

3. Multiply the 1 by the denominator, and add the numerator to find the improper fraction. What is the improper fraction represented by 1.4? _____

Example 5

Write the integer as a ratio of integers and as a decimal.

–4

1. To write –4 as a ratio, write –4 in the numerator and make the denominator 1. Write the ratio. _____

2. To write –4 as a decimal, write a decimal point after the –4, and place a 0 after the decimal point. Write the decimal. _____

Example 6

Is $\sqrt{12}$ rational?

1. Use a calculator. What is $\sqrt{12}$ as a decimal? _____

2. If the decimal terminates or repeats, it is rational. If it does not terminate or repeat, it is irrational. Does the decimal terminate or repeat? _____

3. Is $\sqrt{12}$ rational? _____

Rational Numbers

Name: _____   **Date:** _____

Directions: Write each fraction as a terminating decimal. Show your work.

1. $\frac{4}{5}$ = _____

6. $\frac{1}{2}$ = _____

2. $\frac{1}{10}$ = _____

7. $\frac{3}{5}$ = _____

3. $\frac{7}{8}$ = _____

8. $\frac{7}{10}$ = _____

4. $\frac{3}{4}$ = _____

9. $\frac{5}{8}$ = _____

5. $\frac{1}{8}$ = _____

10. $\frac{1}{5}$ = _____

Name: _____ Date: _____

Directions: Write each fraction as a repeating decimal. Show your work.

1. $\frac{2}{3}$ = _____

2. $\frac{5}{6}$ = _____

3. $\frac{2}{9}$ = _____

4. $\frac{1}{6}$ = _____

5. $\frac{1}{3}$ = _____

6. $\frac{1}{11}$ = _____

7. $\frac{5}{9}$ = _____

8. $\frac{5}{12}$ = _____

9. $\frac{1}{9}$ = _____

10. $\frac{4}{11}$ = _____

Name: _____   Date: _____

Directions: Write each improper fraction as a decimal. Show your work. Then, circle whether it is a terminating or repeating decimal.

1. $\frac{18}{10}$ = _____

terminating   repeating

6. $\frac{8}{3}$ = _____

terminating   repeating

2. $\frac{6}{5}$ = _____

terminating   repeating

7. $\frac{14}{9}$ = _____

terminating   repeating

3. $\frac{4}{3}$ = _____

terminating   repeating

8. $\frac{17}{3}$ = _____

terminating   repeating

4. $\frac{7}{2}$ = _____

terminating   repeating

9. $\frac{16}{5}$ = _____

terminating   repeating

5. $\frac{9}{5}$ = _____

terminating   repeating

10. $\frac{9}{3}$ = _____

terminating   repeating

📝 Reminder

Look at Example 3 on page 21 for a reminder of the steps to change repeating decimals into fractions.

Directions: Write each rational number as a fraction. Show your work.

1. $0.\overline{8}$ = _____

6. $2.\overline{53}$ = _____

2. $0.\overline{16}$ = _____

7. $0.\overline{25}$ = _____

3. $0.\overline{5}$ = _____

8. $3.\overline{95}$ = _____

4. $0.\overline{2}$ = _____

9. $0.\overline{7}$ = _____

5. $1.\overline{26}$ = _____

10. 5.81 = _____

Name: _____ **Date:** _____

> 🖎 **Quick Tip**
>
> Remember, when writing a whole number as a fraction, make the denominator 1.

Directions: Write each number as a fraction.

1. 1.2 = _____

2. 0.75= _____

3. 5.25 = _____

4. −8.4 = _____

5. 12.6 = _____

6. 9 = _____

7. −7 = _____

8. 9.5 = _____

9. 4.08 = _____

10. −5.3 = _____

Name: _____ Date: _____

Directions: Write each integer as a ratio and a decimal.

1. 9
- **a.** Ratio: _____
- **b.** Decimal: _____

2. −11
- **a.** Ratio: _____
- **b.** Decimal: _____

3. 27
- **a.** Ratio: _____
- **b.** Decimal: _____

4. −18
- **a.** Ratio: _____
- **b.** Decimal: _____

5. 100
- **a.** Ratio: _____
- **b.** Decimal: _____

6. −50
- **a.** Ratio: _____
- **b.** Decimal: _____

7. 3
- **a.** Ratio: _____
- **b.** Decimal: _____

8. −8
- **a.** Ratio: _____
- **b.** Decimal: _____

9. 32
- **a.** Ratio: _____
- **b.** Decimal: _____

10. 28
- **a.** Ratio: _____
- **b.** Decimal: _____

Rational Numbers

Name: _____ Date: _____

👉 Quick Tip

For a number to be rational, it must be able to be written as a fraction of two integers (where the denominator is not 0), and it must be a terminating or repeating decimal.

A **square root** is a factor that when multiplied by itself, results in the number under the $\sqrt{}$ symbol. If a number is not a perfect square, its square root is irrational.

Directions: Circle whether each number is rational or irrational. Then, write the reason why each number is rational or irrational.

1. $\sqrt{36}$

rational   irrational

_____

2. $\frac{4}{9}$

rational   irrational

_____

3. π

rational   irrational

_____

4. $\sqrt{5}$

rational   irrational

_____

5. $\sqrt{49}$

rational   irrational

_____

6. $\frac{17}{3}$

rational   irrational

_____

7. $\sqrt{8}$

rational   irrational

_____

8. $\sqrt{11}$

rational   irrational

_____

9. $\frac{15}{8}$

rational   irrational

_____

10. 9.35

rational   irrational

_____

11. $1.\overline{6}$

rational   irrational

_____

12. $\sqrt{45}$

rational   irrational

_____

Name: _____ **Date:** _____

Directions: Write each set of rational numbers in order from least to greatest.

1. $3.5, 3\frac{1}{5}, \frac{-30}{10}, 3\frac{5}{6}$

_____

2. $-8.75, \frac{-80}{5}, -8\frac{3}{6}, -8$

_____

3. $\frac{41}{4}, 10.8, \frac{100}{11}, \frac{21}{2}$

_____

4. $\frac{65}{5}, 13.7, 13\frac{3}{8}, 13.92$

_____

5. $-4.15, \frac{-20}{5}, -4\frac{1}{4}, -4.3$

_____

6. $2\frac{9}{10}, 2.5, \frac{17}{8}, \frac{14}{5}$

_____

7. $-12\frac{1}{4}, -12\frac{3}{5}, -12.95, \frac{-120}{10}$

_____

8. $9\frac{2}{5}, 9.2, 9.75, 9\frac{1}{9}$

_____

9. $7.\overline{6}, 7.83, 7\frac{1}{2}, 7\frac{1}{3}$

_____

10. $-5\frac{2}{3}, -5.14, \frac{-45}{9}, \frac{-41}{7}$

_____

11. $1\frac{7}{8}, 1.\overline{4}, 1\frac{5}{6}, 1.94$

_____

12. $\frac{8}{9}, 0.88886, \frac{7}{8}, \frac{3}{5}$

_____

Name: _____ Date: _____

Directions: Solve each problem.

1. List the rational numbers in order from least to greatest.

$8.2, 8\frac{2}{3}, \frac{43}{5}$

_____

5. List the rational numbers in order from least to greatest.

$10\frac{3}{5}, 10\frac{1}{4}, \frac{109}{10}$

_____

2. List the rational numbers in order from least to greatest.

$3\frac{3}{5}, 3.9, \frac{29}{8}$

_____

6. List the rational numbers in order from least to greatest.

$13\frac{3}{8}, 13.65, \frac{131}{10}$

_____

3. Juno recorded the temperatures for 5 days. He recorded them in the table. List the temperatures in order from coldest to warmest.

_____

Day	Temperature
1	−8.5°
2	−3.9°
3	5°
4	−2.7°
5	1.8°

7. Harvey is doing a group project with two other students. They recorded their data in different ways. Put the data in order from least to greatest.

_____

Data
$70\frac{3}{4}$
70.9
$\frac{351}{5}$

4. Put the rational numbers in order from least to greatest.

$11.5, \frac{95}{8}, 11\frac{1}{4}$

_____

8. Put the rational numbers in order from least to greatest.

$9.5, 9\frac{1}{4}, \frac{99}{10}$

_____

 142250—180 Days of Math

Directions: Plot and label each number on its approximate location on the number line.

1. -9.5; $-9\frac{1}{4}$; $-9\frac{1}{5}$; $\frac{-90}{10}$; $\frac{-29}{3}$

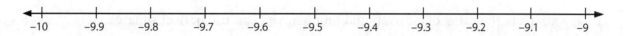

2. $4\frac{3}{8}$; $4\frac{2}{3}$; $\frac{39}{8}$; 4.1; $4\frac{1}{5}$

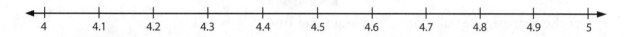

3. -5.8; $-4\frac{3}{5}$; $-5\frac{1}{5}$; $\frac{-25}{6}$; $-5\frac{1}{4}$

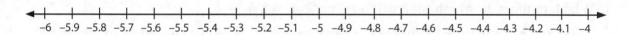

4. $-2\frac{1}{9}$; -1.5; $\frac{0}{7}$; $-1\frac{3}{5}$; $\frac{3}{2}$

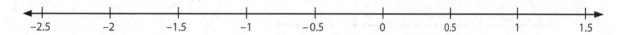

5. $5\frac{4}{5}$; 5; 5.75; $\frac{21}{4}$; $5\frac{2}{9}$

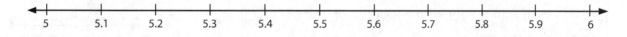

6. $10\frac{7}{8}$; 10.45; $10\frac{3}{4}$; 10.95; $10\frac{2}{5}$

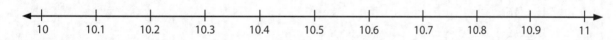

7. -1.95; $-1\frac{5}{6}$; $\frac{-3}{2}$; -1.65; $-1\frac{8}{10}$

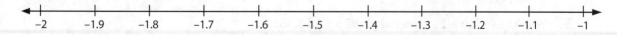

8. $\frac{14}{5}$; 2.75; $\frac{23}{8}$; 2.1; $2\frac{2}{3}$

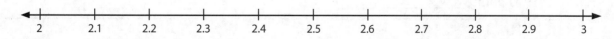

Rational Numbers

Learn about Irrational Numbers

An **irrational number** is a number that cannot be written as a fraction of two integers. Irrational numbers are decimals that do not terminate or repeat.

Examples: π, $\sqrt{3}$

To approximate the value of an irrational number, you can use perfect squares.

A **perfect square** is the product when multiplying an integer by itself.

Examples: $25 = 5^2$, $100 = 10^2$

Example 1

Plot the approximate value of $\sqrt{17}$ on a number line.

1. Find the two perfect squares 17 is between. You can use these to approximate the value of $\sqrt{17}$.

You know $\sqrt{16} = 4$ and $\sqrt{25} = $ _____, so the $\sqrt{17}$ is between 4 and 5.

Which number do you think it will be closer to? Why?

2. You can also use a calculator to approximate $\sqrt{17}$. Round your answer to the nearest hundredth. What is the approximate value of $\sqrt{17}$? _____

3. Locate the approximate value on the number line. Plot and label the point.

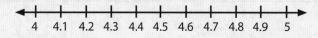

Example 2

Match each square root with a location on the number line.
$\sqrt{13}$, $\sqrt{29}$, $\sqrt{19}$

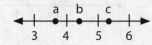

1. List the squares of the whole numbers shown on the number line.

$3^2 = 9$

$4^2 = 16$

$5^2 = 25$

$6^2 = 36$

2. You know that $\sqrt{13}$ is between $\sqrt{9}$ and $\sqrt{16}$.

$\sqrt{13}$ is point a.

3. You know that $\sqrt{29}$ is between $\sqrt{25}$ and $\sqrt{36}$.

$\sqrt{29}$ is point _____.

4. You know that $\sqrt{19}$ is between $\sqrt{16}$ and $\sqrt{25}$.

$\sqrt{19}$ is point _____.

Name: _____ Date: _____

✎ Quick Tip

Remember, rational numbers can be written as a fraction, where the denominator is not 0. Rational numbers also convert to terminating or repeating decimals.

Directions: Circle whether each number is rational or irrational. Then, explain why it is rational or irrational.

1. $\frac{3}{4}$

rational   irrational

_____

_____

2. $5\frac{1}{6}$

rational   irrational

_____

_____

3. $\sqrt{11}$

rational   irrational

_____

_____

4. π

rational   irrational

_____

_____

5. $\sqrt{25}$

rational   irrational

_____

_____

6. $\sqrt{42}$

rational   irrational

_____

_____

7. $\frac{9}{5}$

rational   irrational

_____

_____

8. 2.5

rational   irrational

_____

_____

9. $\sqrt{90}$

rational   irrational

_____

_____

10. $\sqrt{49}$

rational   irrational

_____

_____

Name: _____   Date: _____

Directions: Write the two whole numbers that each square root is between. Circle the number the square root is closer to.

1. $\sqrt{35}$

_____ and _____

2. $\sqrt{11}$

_____ and _____

3. $\sqrt{75}$

_____ and _____

4. $\sqrt{6}$

_____ and _____

5. $\sqrt{88}$

_____ and _____

Directions: Using a calculator, approximate each square root to the nearest hundredth.

6. $\sqrt{41}$

_____

7. $\sqrt{118}$

_____

8. $\sqrt{65}$

_____

9. $\sqrt{59}$

_____

10. $\sqrt{28}$

_____

✏ Hands-On Help

Use a list of perfect squares (or create your own) to help find the approximate values of the square roots.

Directions: Plot and label the approximate location of each square root on the number line.

1. $\sqrt{15}$

6. $\sqrt{78}$

2. $\sqrt{85}$

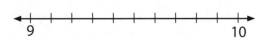

7. $\sqrt{10}$

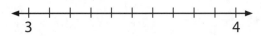

3. $\sqrt{19}$

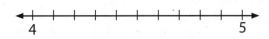

8. $\sqrt{33}$

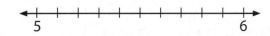

4. $\sqrt{39}$

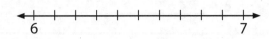

9. $\sqrt{47}$

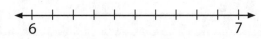

5. $\sqrt{101}$

10. $\sqrt{53}$

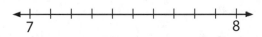

Name: _____   **Date:** _____

Directions: Match the square roots with the locations on the number lines.

1. $\sqrt{47}$, $\sqrt{51}$, $\sqrt{42}$

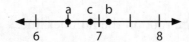

a. _____

b. _____

c. _____

2. $\sqrt{91}$, $\sqrt{75}$, $\sqrt{83}$

a. _____

b. _____

c. _____

3. $\sqrt{48}$, $\sqrt{29}$, $\sqrt{40}$

a. _____

b. _____

c. _____

4. $\sqrt{11}$, $\sqrt{22}$, $\sqrt{18}$

a. _____

b. _____

c. _____

5. $\sqrt{68}$, $\sqrt{63}$, $\sqrt{57}$

a. _____

b. _____

c. _____

6. $\sqrt{44}$, $\sqrt{39}$, $\sqrt{48}$

a. _____

b. _____

c. _____

7. $\sqrt{8}$, $\sqrt{11}$, $\sqrt{6}$

a. _____

b. _____

c. _____

8. $\sqrt{42}$, $\sqrt{47}$, $\sqrt{38}$

a. _____

b. _____

c. _____

Name: _____ Date: _____

Directions: Compare the numbers using >, <, or =.

1. 8.6 _____ $\sqrt{80}$

2. $\sqrt{29}$ _____ $\sqrt{31}$

3. $\frac{9}{2}$ _____ $\sqrt{17}$

4. 10.7 _____ $\sqrt{125}$

5. $\sqrt{2}$ _____ 2.3

6. $\frac{8}{3}$ _____ $\sqrt{5}$

7. −5.3 _____ −$\sqrt{27}$

8. −$\sqrt{11}$ _____ −4

9. −5.2 _____ −$\sqrt{35}$

10. −$3\frac{5}{8}$ _____ −$\sqrt{15}$

11. $\sqrt{45}$ _____ 7.4

12. $\sqrt{10}$ _____ $\frac{7}{2}$

Name: _____ Date: _____

Irrational Numbers

Directions: Order each set of numbers from least to greatest.

1. $\sqrt{101}$, 9.5, $10\frac{9}{10}$, $\sqrt{83}$

_____

7. $\sqrt{120}$, 10.4, $\frac{101}{10}$, $\sqrt{122}$

_____

2. $\sqrt{48}$, 7.5, $\sqrt{42}$, $7\frac{7}{8}$

_____

8. 3.4, $\sqrt{15}$, 4.2, $\sqrt{10}$

_____

3. π, $\sqrt{15}$, $3\frac{1}{8}$, $\frac{16}{5}$

_____

9. $\frac{43}{5}$, 8, $\sqrt{62}$, 7.6

_____

4. $\sqrt{63}$, 8.7, $7\frac{1}{10}$, $\sqrt{65}$

_____

10. $\sqrt{55}$, 6.3, $\sqrt{60}$, 7.1

_____

5. $5\frac{1}{3}$, $\sqrt{35}$, 5.6, $\sqrt{39}$

_____

11. $\sqrt{102}$, 10.9, $10\frac{8}{9}$, $\sqrt{99}$

_____

6. $\sqrt{71}$, 8.9, $\sqrt{65}$, $\sqrt{78}$

_____

12. $\sqrt{7}$, 2.9, $\frac{14}{5}$, $\sqrt{11}$

_____

Math Talk

What strategies and reasoning did you use to order these numbers?

Name: _____   Date: _____

Directions: Circle the larger number in each problem. You can use a calculator to help you.

1. $2.\overline{6}$ or $\sqrt{8}$

7. $\sqrt{118}$ or 11.1

2. $\sqrt{15}$ or 3.9

8. $3\frac{1}{8}$ or $\sqrt{10}$

3. 9.2 or $\sqrt{82}$

9. $\sqrt{39}$ or 6.5

4. $\sqrt{51}$ or 7.8

10. $\frac{76}{10}$ or $\sqrt{51}$

5. $10\frac{1}{5}$ or $\sqrt{108}$

11. $9.\overline{3}$ or $\sqrt{86}$

6. π or $\sqrt{8}$

12. $\frac{38}{9}$ or $\sqrt{20}$

Name: _____   **Date:** _____

Directions: Estimate a decimal approximation for each equation. Round each answer to the nearest hundredth.

1. $5 + \sqrt{8} =$ _____

2. $3\pi =$ _____

3. $5\sqrt{4} =$ _____

4. $2\sqrt{5} + 6 =$ _____

5. $10 - \sqrt{3} =$ _____

6. $\sqrt{12} + 8 =$ _____

7. $4\sqrt{10} =$ _____

8. $5 + \sqrt{15} =$ _____

9. $6\sqrt{20} =$ _____

10. $7 + \sqrt{24} =$ _____

11. $3\sqrt{18} =$ _____

12. $8\pi =$ _____

13. $\sqrt{73} + 4 =$ _____

14. $2\sqrt{9} =$ _____

Name: _____ Date: _____

Directions: Estimate a decimal approximation for each equation. Round the answer to the nearest hundredth. Then, plot the answer on the number line.

1. $2 + \sqrt{6}$ = _____

4   5

6. 3π = _____

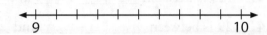

9   10

2. $3\sqrt{7}$ = _____

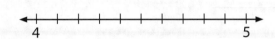

7   8

7. $12 - \sqrt{76}$ = _____

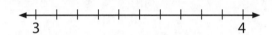

3   4

3. $\sqrt{51} + 3$ = _____

10   11

8. $2\sqrt{23}$ = _____

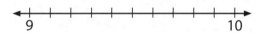

9   10

4. $8 - \sqrt{18}$ = _____

3   4

9. $4 + \sqrt{5}$ = _____

6   7

5. $2\sqrt{22}$ = _____

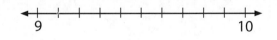

9   10

10. $\sqrt{10} + 5$ = _____

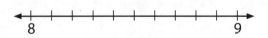

8   9

Name: _____   **Date:** _____

Directions: Write the two numbers that each square root is between.

1. $\sqrt{15}$ is between _____ and _____.

2. $\sqrt{84}$ is between _____ and _____.

3. $\sqrt{115}$ is between _____ and _____.

4. $\sqrt{29}$ is between _____ and _____.

Directions: Match each square root with its location on the number line.

5. $\sqrt{66}$, $\sqrt{52}$, $\sqrt{57}$

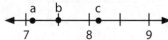

   a. _____

   b. _____

   c. _____

6. $\sqrt{105}$, $\sqrt{99}$, $\sqrt{110}$

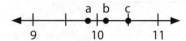

   a. _____

   b. _____

   c. _____

Directions: Plot the approximate value of the square root on the number line for each problem.

7. $\sqrt{65}$

9. $\sqrt{10}$

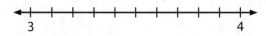

8. $\sqrt{98}$

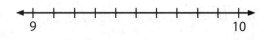

10. $\sqrt{52}$

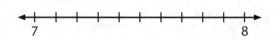

Directions: Solve each problem.

1. Write the numbers from least to greatest.
   $\sqrt{17}$, 4.5, $\sqrt{32}$, 6.4

   _____

2. Circle the larger number.
   $\sqrt{110}$ or 10.1

3. Compare the numbers using >, <, or =.
   −6.3 _____ −$\sqrt{36}$

4. Write $\frac{1}{8}$ as a decimal.

   _____

5. Write the numbers in order from least to greatest.

   7.3, $\frac{37}{5}$, $7\frac{8}{9}$, $\frac{40}{5}$

   _____

6. Write $\frac{21}{4}$ as a decimal.

   _____

7. Is $\frac{1}{9}$ a terminating or repeating decimal?

   _____

8. Which two consecutive integers is $\sqrt{53}$ between?

   _____ and _____

9. Write −3 as a ratio of integers.

   _____

10. Is $\frac{4}{5}$ a rational number?
    yes   no

Spiral Review

Name: _____ Date: _____

Directions: Solve each problem.

1. Plot the approximate location of $\sqrt{77}$ on the number line. Use a calculator.

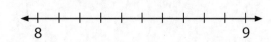

2. Plot each number on the number line. Use a calculator.

$\sqrt{21}$; $\sqrt{19}$; $\sqrt{24}$

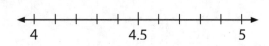

3. Write −4 as a decimal.

_____

4. Write the numbers in order from least to greatest.

$8\frac{5}{9}$, 8.75 , $\frac{41}{5}$, 8.9

_____

5. Is $\frac{3}{5}$ a terminating or repeating decimal?

_____

6. Write $0.\overline{2}$ as a fraction.

_____

7. Write each number as a fraction.

a. 6.4 = _____

b. −8 = _____

c. 0.23 = _____

8. Write π as a decimal approximation to the nearest hundredth.

_____

9. Compare using > or <.

$\sqrt{55}$ _____ $\sqrt{48}$

10. Write an example of an irrational number.

_____

Directions: Solve each problem. Use a calculator when asked for decimal approximations of square roots.

1. Match each number with its location on the number line.

$\sqrt{35}$, 6.5, $\sqrt{40}$

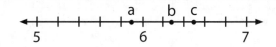

a. _____

b. _____

c. _____

2. Write an example of a whole number.

_____

3. Graph the numbers on the number line.
$\sqrt{31}$, $\sqrt{27}$, $\sqrt{39}$

4. Write $0.\overline{45}$ as a fraction.

_____

5. Write $1\frac{7}{8}$ as a decimal.

_____

6. Graph $\sqrt{51}$ on the number line.

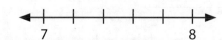

7. Circle the larger number.

$\sqrt{76}$ or $8\frac{1}{5}$

8. Is $\frac{15}{4}$ a terminating or repeating decimal?

_____

9. Plot the approximate decimal value of $6 \times \sqrt{46}$.

10. Order the numbers from least to greatest.

$-4\frac{1}{4}$, -4.2, $\frac{-9}{2}$, -4.67

_____

Spiral Review

Name: _____   Date: _____

Directions: Solve each problem. Use a calculator when asked for decimal approximations of square roots.

1. Write an example of an integer.

_____

2. Write $\frac{7}{5}$ as a decimal.

_____

3. Plot the decimal approximation of $\sqrt{7}$ on the number line.

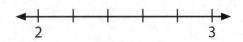

4. Match each number with its location on the number line.

$4\frac{3}{8}$, $\sqrt{17}$, 4.8

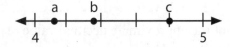

    a. _____

    b. _____

    c. _____

5. What is the decimal approximation for $\sqrt{61}$?

_____

6. Write $\frac{21}{5}$ as a decimal.

_____

7. Write 8.2 as a ratio of integers.

_____

8. $\sqrt{49}$ = _____

9. What is $9 - \sqrt{5}$, rounded to the nearest hundredth?

_____

10. Write $0.\overline{7}$ as a fraction.

_____

Directions: Solve each problem. Use a calculator when asked for decimal approximations of square roots.

1. Plot the decimal approximation of $\sqrt{41}$ on the number line.

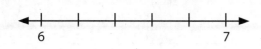

2. Plot and label the approximate locations of the numbers on the number line.

$\sqrt{6}, \sqrt{14}, \sqrt{10}$

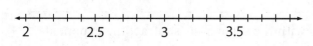

3. Write a decimal approximation of $\sqrt{83} + 11$. Round to the nearest hundredth.

_____

4. Write 26 as a ratio.

_____

5. Write $0.\overline{35}$ as a fraction.

_____

6. Match each number with its location on the number line.

$\sqrt{59}$, $7\frac{1}{4}$, 7.01

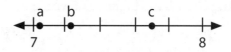

a. _____

b. _____

c. _____

7. Write these numbers in order from least to greatest.

$9\frac{3}{8}$, 8.98, $\sqrt{144}$

_____

8. Plot the decimal approximation of $\sqrt{118}$ on the number line.

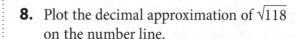

9. Is π rational or irrational? Why?

_____

10. Compare the numbers using >, <, or =.

$\sqrt{37}$ _____ 7.1

Spiral Review

Learn about Exponents

Exponents are used to show the number of times a number is multiplied by itself.

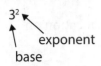

For example, $3^2 = 3 \times 3$ and $3 \times 3 = 9$.

Exponent Rules

The Zero Exponent Rule: any number to the 0 power is equal to 1.

Example: $4^0 = 1$

The Identity Exponent Rule: any number to the first power is equal to the base.

Example: $5^1 = 5$

The Product Rule: when multiplying two numbers with the same base, add the exponents.

Example: $x^3 \cdot x^2 = x^5$ because $(x \cdot x \cdot x) \times (x \cdot x) = x^5$

The Quotient Rule: when dividing two numbers with the same base, subtract the exponents.

Example: $\dfrac{x^5}{x^4} = x^1$ because $\dfrac{x \cdot x \cdot x \cdot x \cdot x}{x \cdot x \cdot x \cdot x} = x$

The Negative Exponent Rule: when there is a negative exponent, find the reciprocal of the number to make the exponent positive.

Example: $x^{-2} = \dfrac{1}{x^2}$

The Power of a Power Exponent Rule: when raising a power to a power, you multiply the exponents.

Example: $(x^4)^3 = x^{12}$ because $(x \cdot x \cdot x \cdot x)(x \cdot x \cdot x \cdot x)(x \cdot x \cdot x \cdot x) = x^{12}$

The Power of a Product Exponent Rule: when raising a product to a power, you multiply the power outside the parentheses by each of the powers inside the parentheses.

Example: $(x^2 y^3)^5 = x^{10} y^{15}$

The Power of a Quotient Exponent Rule: when raising a quotient to a power, you multiply the power outside of the parentheses by each power inside the parentheses.

Example: $\left(\dfrac{x^2}{y^3} \right)^4 = \dfrac{x^8}{y^{12}}$

📝 Reminder

Remember, any number to the 0 power is equal to 1. Any number to the first power is equal to the base. When multiplying numbers with the same base, add the exponents.

Directions: Solve each problem.

1. $5^0 = $ _____

2. $f^1 = $ _____

3. $g^3 \cdot g^4 = $ _____

4. $k^5 \cdot k^6 = $ _____

5. $y^1 = $ _____

6. $m^0 = $ _____

7. $w^9 \cdot w^3 = $ _____

8. $7^0 = $ _____

9. $q^5 \cdot q^2 \cdot q^3 = $ _____

10. $b^{-3} \cdot b^5 = $ _____

11. $4^2 \cdot 4^3 = $ _____

12. $6^1 = $ _____

Exponents

Name: _____   Date: _____

> ### 📝 Reminder
>
> When dividing numbers with the same base, subtract the exponents.
>
> Example: $\dfrac{t^6 w^7}{t^2 w^4} = t^4 w^3$
>
> When raising a quotient to a power, multiply the exponent outside the parentheses by each exponent inside.
>
> Example: $\left(\dfrac{m^6}{n^4}\right)^2 = \dfrac{m^{12}}{n^8}$

Directions: Solve each problem.

1. $\dfrac{y^4}{y^2} = $ _____

2. $\dfrac{a^2 b^5}{a\, b^3} = $ _____

3. $\dfrac{4^3}{4^2} = $ _____

4. $\dfrac{h^8}{h^5} = $ _____

5. $\dfrac{7^7}{7^4} = $ _____

6. $\left(\dfrac{w^9}{x^3}\right)^2 = $ _____

7. $\dfrac{x^3 y^4 z^5}{x y^2 z^2} = $ _____

8. $\dfrac{9^5}{9^3} = $ _____

9. $\dfrac{p^{18}}{p^{10}} = $ _____

10. $\dfrac{j^3 k^8}{j^2 k} = $ _____

11. $\dfrac{6^2}{6^1} = $ _____

12. $\left(\dfrac{k^5}{m^3}\right)^3 = $ _____

Reminder

When raising a power to a power, multiply the exponents. Example: $(2^2)^3 = 2^6 = 64$

When finding the power of a product, multiply the exponent outside the parentheses by each number inside the parentheses. Example: $(g^3h^4)^3 = g^9h^{12}$

Directions: Solve each problem.

1. $(m^4)^3 =$ _____

2. $(a^4b^3)^5 =$ _____

3. $(4^2)^2 =$ _____

4. $(x^6)^7 =$ _____

5. $(w^2y^3)^2 =$ _____

6. $(h^3)^9 =$ _____

7. $(b^4c^2)^4 =$ _____

8. $(z^7)^9 =$ _____

9. $(8^2)^0 =$ _____

10. $(p^5q^2)^6 =$ _____

11. $(3^2)^2 =$ _____

12. $(x^5y^2)^8 =$ _____

Exponents

Name: _____ Date: _____

Example

$\dfrac{x^3}{x^5} = x^{-2}$, so you write it as $\dfrac{1}{x^2}$.

Directions: Solve each problem. Write all answers with positive exponents.

1. $d^{-2} =$ _____

2. $5^{-3} =$ _____

3. $\dfrac{x^3}{x^9} =$ _____

4. $\dfrac{4^3}{4^5} =$ _____

5. $7^{-2} =$ _____

6. $\dfrac{a^5}{a^9} =$ _____

7. $\dfrac{m^3 n^4}{m^7 n^2} =$ _____

8. $\dfrac{w^5}{w^{11}} =$ _____

9. $\dfrac{p^9}{p^{12}} =$ _____

10. $8^{-3} =$ _____

11. $\dfrac{h^9}{h^{14}} =$ _____

12. $\dfrac{x^2 y^{10}}{x^3 y^9} =$ _____

 142250—180 Days of Math

Directions: Solve each problem.

1. $f^0 =$ _____

2. $t^1 =$ _____

3. $g^5 \cdot g^7 =$ _____

4. $(y^6)^9 =$ _____

5. $4^2 \cdot 4^1 =$ _____

6. $\left(\dfrac{m^4}{n^3}\right)^5 =$ _____

7. $(5^2)^2 =$ _____

8. $\dfrac{y^7}{y^5} =$ _____

9. $x^3 y^2 \cdot x^4 y^3 =$ _____

10. $k^1 =$ _____

11. $p^{-5} =$ _____

12. $f^3 \cdot f^5 =$ _____

Exponents

Math Talk

How did the exponent rules help you solve the problems on this page?

Learn about Square Roots and Cube Roots
Words to Know

- When you **square** a number, you are raising it to the power of 2. Example: $3^2 = 3 \times 3 = 9$

- When you **cube** a number, you are raising it to the power of 3. Example: $2^3 = 2 \times 2 \times 2 = 8$

- The **square root** of a number is a number that when multiplied by itself, results in the number under the square root symbol. Example: $\sqrt{25} = 5$, because $5 \times 5 = 25$.

- The **cube root** of a number is a number that when cubed results in the number under the cube root symbol. Example: $\sqrt[3]{8} = 2$, because $2 \times 2 \times 2 = 8$.

- **Perfect squares** are numbers with whole number square roots. Examples of perfect squares are 4, because $\sqrt{4} = 2$, and 9, because $\sqrt{9} = 3$.

- **Perfect cubes** are numbers with whole number cube roots. Examples of perfect cubes are 8, because $\sqrt[3]{8} = 2$, and 27, because $\sqrt[3]{27} = 3$.

Any square root that is not a perfect square is an irrational number. Examples of irrational numbers are $\sqrt{2}$ and $\sqrt{21}$.

Example 1

What is $\sqrt{x^2}$?

1. Think about what you can multiply by itself to get x^2. Because $x \cdot x = x^2$, the solution is x.

Example 2

Solve $x^2 = 16$.

1. Take the square root of both sides of the equation.

$\sqrt{x^2} = x$

$\sqrt{16} = 4$

2. So, $x = 4$.

Example 3

Solve $x^3 = 8$.

1. Take the cube root of both sides of the equation.

$\sqrt[3]{x^3} = x$

$\sqrt[3]{8} = 2$

2. So, $x = 2$.

Name: _____ **Date:** _____

Directions: Solve each problem.

1. $4^2 =$ _____

2. $5^3 =$ _____

3. $1^2 =$ _____

4. $9^2 =$ _____

5. $7^3 =$ _____

6. $3^3 =$ _____

7. $8^2 =$ _____

8. $5^2 =$ _____

9. $11^2 =$ _____

10. $6^3 =$ _____

11. $4^3 =$ _____

12. $2^2 =$ _____

13. $7^2 =$ _____

14. $10^3 =$ _____

Square Roots and Cube Roots

Name: _____ Date: _____

✎ Hands-On Help

Use a list of perfect squares to help you, or create your own for easy reference.

Directions: Find the square root of each number.

1. $\sqrt{144}$ = _____

2. $\sqrt{a^2}$ = _____

3. $\sqrt{x^2 y^2}$ = _____

4. $\sqrt{64}$ = _____

5. $\sqrt{121}$ = _____

6. $\sqrt{m^2}$ = _____

7. $\sqrt{9}$ = _____

8. $\sqrt{81}$ = _____

9. $\sqrt{g^2}$ = _____

10. $\sqrt{a^2 b^2}$ = _____

11. $\sqrt{100}$ = _____

12. $\sqrt{\frac{1}{4}}$ = _____

Math Talk

What reasoning did you use to solve question 12?

📝 Hands-On Help

Use a list of perfect cubes to help you, or create your own for easy reference.

Directions: Find the cube root of each number.

1. $\sqrt[3]{125} =$ _____

2. $\sqrt[3]{x^3} =$ _____

3. $\sqrt[3]{64} =$ _____

4. $\sqrt[3]{27} =$ _____

5. $\sqrt[3]{216} =$ _____

6. $\sqrt[3]{a^3} =$ _____

7. $\sqrt[3]{512} =$ _____

8. $\sqrt[3]{1} =$ _____

9. $\sqrt[3]{729} =$ _____

10. $\sqrt[3]{g^3 h^3} =$ _____

11. $\sqrt[3]{8} =$ _____

12. $\sqrt[3]{1000} =$ _____

Math Talk

How does the size of a cube root compare to the size of a square root of the same number?

Name: _____ Date: _____

Directions: Solve for x.

1. $x^2 = 49$

$x =$ _____

2. $\sqrt{x^3} = 64$

$x =$ _____

3. $x^3 = 1,000$

$x =$ _____

4. $x^2 = 121$

$x =$ _____

5. $x^2 = 1$

$x =$ _____

6. $x^3 = 216$

$x =$ _____

7. $x^3 = 125$

$x =$ _____

8. $x^2 = 4$

$x =$ _____

9. $x^2 = 169$

$x =$ _____

10. $x^3 = 27$

$x =$ _____

11. $x^2 = 225$

$x =$ _____

12. $x^3 = 343$

$x =$ _____

Math Talk

How can prime factorization help you find the square root or cube root of a number?

Name: _____ **Date:** _____

Directions: Solve each problem.

1. $7^3 =$ _____

2. $20^2 =$ _____

3. $16^2 =$ _____

4. $2^3 =$ _____

5. $(\frac{1}{2})^2 =$ _____

6. $\sqrt{100} =$ _____

7. $\sqrt{w^2} =$ _____

8. $\sqrt[3]{1,000} =$ _____

9. $\sqrt[3]{1} =$ _____

10. $x^2 = 1$

    $x =$ _____

11. $x^2 = 36$

    $x =$ _____

12. $x^3 = 64$

    $x =$ _____

13. $x^3 = 216$

    $x =$ _____

14. $x^2 = 49$

    $x =$ _____

Square Roots and Cube Roots

Math Talk

Why do you think they are called *square* root and *cube* root?

Learn about Multistep Problem Solving

To solve problems with multiple operations, follow the **Order of Operations**.

Step 1: Solve any problems inside grouping symbols. { }, [ ], ( ), or | |

Step 2: Simplify any exponents.

Step 3: Solve all multiplication and division, working from left to right.

Step 4: Solve all addition and subtraction, working from left to right.

Example 1

Solve.

$4[9 + 3(4 - 6)] + 3^2$

Follow the order of operations to solve the problem. Follow the steps.

$$4[9 + 3(4 - 6)] + 3^2$$

1. $4[9 + 3\,(-2\,)] + 3^2$
2. $4[9 + (-6)] + 3^2$
3. $4[3] + 3^2$
4. $4[3] + 9$
5. $12 + 9$
6. $\boxed{21}$

Example 2

A cube has a volume of 729 cubic inches. What is the length of each side?

1. On a cube, all sides are equal, and volume = length × width × height. So, you can find the cube root of 729 to find the length of one side. What is $\sqrt[3]{729}$?

2. Find the answer using prime factorization. Follow the steps.

$x^3 = 729$
$x = \sqrt[3]{729}$

$9^3 = 729$
$x = 9$

$9 \times 9 \times 9 = 9^3 = 729$

$x =$ _____

3. You can also solve or check your answer with a calculator.

🐾 Quick Tip

When calculating more than one exponent in the same problem, always find the exponent value first, then add or subtract the products.

Directions: Solve each problem.

1. $3^3 =$ _____

2. $8^2 =$ _____

3. $5^3 =$ _____

4. $1^8 =$ _____

5. $2^4 =$ _____

6. $6^2 + 3^2 =$ _____

7. $7^3 - 4^2 =$ _____

8. $4^4 + 2^3 =$ _____

9. $5^1 + 3^4 =$ _____

10. $6^2 + 9^2 =$ _____

11. $2^0 + 8^3 - 3^2 =$ _____

12. $7^2 - 5^2 =$ _____

13. $1^4 + 4^2 - 3^2 =$ _____

14. $9^3 - 8^2 + 7^1 =$ _____

Name: _____ Date: _____

🖎 Quick Tip

When calculating more than one **radical** (a square or cube root) in the same problem, always find the value of all the radicals first, then add or subtract the answers.

Directions: Solve each problem.

1. $\sqrt{81} =$ _____

2. $\sqrt[3]{64} =$ _____

3. $\sqrt{25} =$ _____

4. $\sqrt{4} =$ _____

5. $\sqrt[3]{125} =$ _____

6. $\sqrt{49} + \sqrt{36} =$ _____

7. $\sqrt[3]{216} - \sqrt{9} =$ _____

8. $\sqrt{144} + \sqrt{1} =$ _____

9. $\sqrt{100} - \sqrt{64} =$ _____

10. $\sqrt[3]{343} + \sqrt[3]{8} =$ _____

11. $\sqrt{36} + \sqrt{4} =$ _____

12. $\sqrt[3]{512} + \sqrt{16} =$ _____

Directions: Solve each problem using the order of operations.

1. $(\frac{1}{3})^2 + \sqrt{(2^2 + 12)} =$ _____

2. $\frac{1}{2}(5^2 - 3^2) + (9 - 2^2) =$ _____

3. $(\frac{1}{2})^3 + 3(6^2 - 8) =$ _____

4. $-3[\,2(8 - 9) + 3(-4 - 1)] =$ _____

5. $\sqrt[3]{64} - \sqrt{9} + 2(-5 + 6) =$ _____

6. $8[9 - (8 - 10) + 6] - 10\frac{3}{4} =$ _____

7. $\frac{3}{8}(2^3) - 7 + 2(9 - 11) =$ _____

8. $\sqrt{(10^2 - 6^2)} + 3(-6 - 4) =$ _____

9. $(\sqrt{\frac{1}{4}})^3 \times 16 - 5[6 - (-2)] =$ _____

10. $\sqrt[3]{216} - \sqrt{16} + \frac{3}{5}(15) =$ _____

11. $(\frac{3}{4})^2 \times 32 - \sqrt{9} + 8(3 - 5) =$ _____

12. $4 - 2(9 - 7) + \sqrt[3]{27} - \sqrt{4} =$ _____

Multistep Problem Solving

Name: _____ **Date:** _____

Directions: Solve each problem. Label your answers with the correct units.

1. Marcy is buying a new square rug for her room. The area of the rug is 64 square feet. How long is each side of the rug?

_____

2. Kiva needs to make a cover for her square-shaped pool. The area of the top of the pool is 121 square feet. How long should Kiva make each side of the pool cover?

_____

3. Amaya is building a cube for her math project. The cube needs to have a volume of 125 cubic centimeters. How long should Amaya make each side of the cube?

_____

4. Eder is painting a square wall that covers 100 square yards. What is the length of the wall?

_____

5. Marquis bought a box of stuffing to make pillows. The volume of the box is 512 cubic inches. What is the length of one side of the box?

_____

6. Rashad bought a picture for his bedroom wall. The square picture has an area of 144 square centimeters. What is the length of one side of the picture?

_____

7. Kaia bought a box of marbles with a volume of 729 cubic centimeters. The box is in the shape of a cube. What is the length of one side of the box?

_____

8. Keisha is building a square-shaped fence for her dog to play in. The area of the fence is 49 square meters. What is the length of one side of the fence?

_____

9. Idris is making a cube sculpture for her art class. The volume of her sculpture is 343 cubic centimeters. What is the length of one side of the sculpture?

_____

10. Dia's parents are making a square-shaped track for her to ride her bike around in the backyard. The area of the track is 144 square meters. How long is one side of the track?

_____

Directions: Solve each problem.

1. $5^3 - 3^4 =$ _____

2. $2^4 + 6^2 =$ _____

3. $3^0 + 4^2 - 1^2 =$ _____

4. $8^2 - 7^2 =$ _____

5. $\sqrt[3]{8} + \sqrt{4} =$ _____

6. $\sqrt{81} - \sqrt{49} =$ _____

7. $\sqrt[3]{27} + \sqrt{121} =$ _____

8. $(\frac{1}{4})^2 \times 48 + 9(-5 - 6) =$ _____

9. $\sqrt{144} - 6(-5 + 7) - 4^2 =$ _____

10. $7[-6(5 - 3) + 4(2 - 4)] + 5^2 =$ _____

11. A cube has a volume of 1,000 cubic inches. What is the length of one side?

_____

12. A square rug has an area of 169 cubic feet. What is the length of one side?

_____

Learn about Scientific Notation

Scientific notation is used to write very large or very small numbers.

- To write a number in scientific notation, move the decimal point until there is only one nonzero digit to the left of the decimal point. Rewrite the number as being multiplied by 10 with an exponent equal to the number of places the decimal was moved.

- If the original number is greater than 1, the exponent will be positive. If the original number is less than 1, the exponent will be negative.

- When moving the decimal one space to the left, add 1 to the exponent.

- When moving the decimal one space to the right, subtract 1 from the exponent.

Example 1

Write 8,700,000 in scientific notation.

1. Move the decimal point to the left until there is one nonzero digit to the left of the decimal point.

   8 700 000,

   How many places did you move the decimal point? _____

2. Write the nonzero digits, with the decimal point between them, and drop the zeroes. The exponent is positive because the original number is greater than 1. The number of places the decimal was moved becomes the exponent.

   $8,700,000 = 8.7 \times 10^6$

Example 2

Write 0.00058 in scientific notation.

1. Move the decimal point to the right until there is only one nonzero digit to the left of the decimal.

   0.00058

   How many places did you move the decimal point? _____

2. Write the nonzero digits, with the decimal point between them, and drop the zeroes. The exponent is negative because the original number is less than 1. The number of places the decimal was moved becomes the exponent.

   $0.00058 = 5.8 \times 10^{-4}$

Example 3

Write 5.2×10^5 in standard form.

1. The exponent of 5 tells us to move the decimal point to the right 5 places. Add zeroes when necessary. So, in standard form, the number is 520,000.

Learn about Scientific Notation *(cont.)*

Example 4

Add. Write the final answer in scientific notation.

$(3.5 \times 10^4) + (2.6 \times 10^5)$

1. Rewrite one of the numbers so the exponents are the same. You can rewrite the first number so the exponent is 5. Moving the decimal one place to the left will add 1 to the exponent.

   $(0.35 \times 10^5) + (2.6 \times 10^5)$

2. Now, add the decimals.

   $0.35 + 2.6 =$ _____

3. The answer is 2.95×10^5.

Example 5

Multiply. Write the final answer in scientific notation.

$(1.5 \times 10^3)(2.1 \times 10^2)$

1. First, multiply. $1.5 \times 2.1 =$ _____

2. Next, add the exponents. $3 + 2 =$ _____

3. The answer is 3.15×10^5.

Example 6

Divide. Write the final answer in scientific notation.

$\dfrac{(8.2 \times 10^6)}{(4.1 \times 10^5)}$

1. Divide. $8.2 \div 4.1 =$ _____

2. Next, subtract the exponents. $6 - 5 =$ _____

3. The answer is 2×10^1.

Name: _____ Date: _____

Directions: Write each number in scientific notation.

1. 540,000,000

_____

2. 1,800

_____

3. 0.00000089

_____

4. 6,700,000,000

_____

5. 0.0000000032

_____

6. 87,000

_____

7. 0.00045

_____

8. 0.000051

_____

9. 0.0068

_____

10. 2,300,000,000,000

_____

11. 65,000,000

_____

12. 0.000000035

_____

13. 0.053

_____

14. 6,030,000

_____

Name: _____ Date: _____

Directions: Write each number in standard form.

1. 1.2×10^5

_____

2. 3.6×10^{-4}

_____

3. 8.7×10^3

_____

4. 6.6×10^{-8}

_____

5. 5.8×10^{-5}

_____

6. 8.3×10^{-3}

_____

7. 7.4×10^7

_____

8. 1.8×10^{-2}

_____

9. 3.9×10^4

_____

10. 2.4×10^3

_____

11. 8.3×10^{-9}

_____

12. 6.2×10^6

_____

13. 9.1×10^{-1}

_____

14. 4.7×10^8

_____

Name: _____   **Date:** _____

🖎 Quick Tip

Remember, you can only add or subtract numbers when the exponents are the same. If they are not the same, rewrite one of the numbers.

Directions: Add or subtract using scientific notation.

1. $(4.2 \times 10^4) + (2.3 \times 10^4) =$ _____

2. $(8.6 \times 10^{-5}) - (7.2 \times 10^{-5}) =$ _____

3. $(4.3 \times 10^2) + (3.6 \times 10^3) =$ _____

4. $(9.5 \times 10^7) - (6.2 \times 10^6) =$ _____

5. $(7.3 \times 10^{-6}) - (3.6 \times 10^{-7}) =$ _____

6. $(5.9 \times 10^8) + (6.8 \times 10^9) =$ _____

7. $(1.9 \times 10^{-5}) - (1.4 \times 10^{-5}) =$ _____

8. $(6.4 \times 10^{-4}) + (8.4 \times 10^{-4}) =$ _____

9. $(2.9 \times 10^3) + (5.4 \times 10^4) =$ _____

10. $(4.4 \times 10^6) - (3.3 \times 10^6) =$ _____

11. $(7.8 \times 10^9) + (1.6 \times 10^{10}) =$ _____

12. $(3.8 \times 10^{-3}) - (2.5 \times 10^{-5}) =$ _____

Directions: Multiply or divide using scientific notation. Be sure that your final answers are in scientific notation.

1. $(4.1 \times 10^6)\,(2.3 \times 10^4) =$ _____

2. $(1.9 \times 10^{-3})\,(3.4 \times 10^{-8}) =$ _____

3. $(8.5 \times 10^5)\,(4.1 \times 10^3) =$ _____

4. $(9.4 \times 10^{-8})\,(6.5 \times 10^{-4}) =$ _____

5. $(5.9 \times 10^2)\,(6.1 \times 10^4) =$ _____

6. $(7.3 \times 10^{-5})\,(2.1 \times 10^3) =$ _____

7. $\dfrac{(3.1 \times 10^6)}{(1.24 \times 10^3)} =$ _____

8. $\dfrac{(8.8 \times 10^{-5})}{(2.2 \times 10^{-4})} =$ _____

9. $\dfrac{(4.36 \times 10^9)}{(1.09 \times 10^{-3})} =$ _____

10. $\dfrac{(2.64 \times 10^3)}{(2.2 \times 10^2)} =$ _____

11. $\dfrac{(5.306 \times 10^7)}{(3.79 \times 10^{-9})} =$ _____

12. $\dfrac{(9.1 \times 10^{-8})}{(1.4 \times 10^2)} =$ _____

Scientific Notation

Name: _____ Date: _____

Directions: Solve each problem. Be sure to write your answers in scientific notation unless otherwise stated.

1. A farmer's field has a length of 4.3×10^3 yards and a width of 2.1×10^4 yards. What is the area of the farmer's field?

   _____

2. From over a span of two years, 1.8×10^{12} tons of strawberries were produced in the United States. Over the next two years, 1.3×10^{12} tons of strawberries were produced in the United States. How many more strawberries were produced in the first two years?

   _____

3. Jupiter is 4.681×10^8 miles from the sun. Earth is 9.3×10^7 miles from the sun. How much farther from the sun is Jupiter compared to Earth?

   _____

4. One cup of water has 8.36×10^{24} molecules of water. How many molecules would be in 3 cups of water?

   _____

5. Light travels at 3.0×10^8 meters per second. Sound travels at 3.4×10^8 meters per second. How much faster does sound travel?

   _____

6. The diameter of a grain of sand is 2.4×10^{-3} inches. Write this number in standard form.

   _____

7. The thickness of a sheet of paper is 0.004 inches. Write this number in scientific notation.

   _____

8. The weight of an elephant is 7.23×10^7 ounces. What is the weight of 4 elephants in scientific notation?

   _____

9. The weight of a loaded truck is 1.2×10^4 kilograms. Another truck weighs 2.5×10^4 kilograms. How much more does the heavier truck weigh?

   _____

10. Using the same information from question 9, what is the total weight of the trucks?

   _____

Learn about Proportional Relationships and Slope

In a **proportional relationship**, the values of one variable are multiplied by the same number to get the values of the other variable. The number you multiply by is called the **constant of proportionality**.

The graph of a proportional relationship must pass through the origin (0, 0).

The unit rate in a proportional relationship is also the slope of the line.

Example 1

Maxine is making a poetry book. She can fit 4 poems on each page. There is a proportional relationship between the number of pages in the book and the number of poems. Graph the relationship, and answer the question.

1. For every 1 page, there are 4 poems. This tells us that as the x-value increases by 1, the y-value increases by 4. This is the unit rate. The information given also tells us the slant, or steepness, of the line. The steepness of a line is also known as the **slope**.

Number of Pages	1	2	3	4
Number of Poems	4	8	12	26

2. What is the slope of the line? How much does the line go up each time it goes over 1 to the right? It goes up by 4. So, the slope is $\frac{4}{1}$.

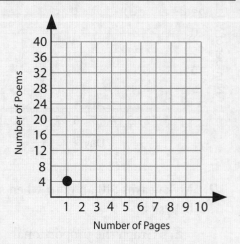

Example 2

Find the slope of side *AB* of the triangle.

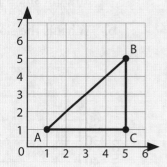

1. Find the coordinates of point *A* and point *B*.

   What are the coordinates of point *A*? _____

   What are the coordinates of point *B*? _____

2. Subtract the y-values in the numerator and the corresponding x-values in the denominator using the formula: $\frac{y_2 - y_1}{x_2 - x_1}$

   What is $y_2 - y_1$?

   $5 - 1 = 4$

   What is $x_2 - x_1$?

   $5 - 1 = 4$

3. Write your answer as a fraction. What is the slope? The slope is $\frac{4}{4}$, which reduces to $\frac{1}{1}$.

Name: _____   Date: _____

Directions: Solve each problem.

1. Javier runs 5 miles each day.

   a. Graph the proportional relationship between the number of days Javier runs and the total number of miles he runs.

   b. What is the slope of the line?

   _____

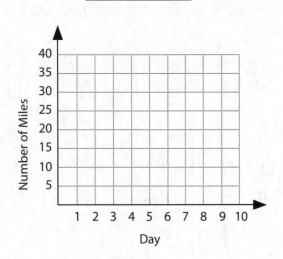

2. Myka earns $10 an hour when she babysits.

   a. Graph the proportional relationship between the number of hours Myka babysits and the amount she is paid.

   b. What is the slope of the line?

   _____

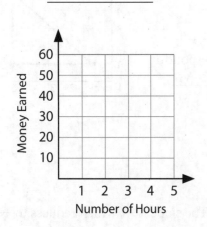

3. Jenika planted 2 tomato plants in each row of her garden.

   a. Graph the proportional relationship between the number of rows in Jenika's garden and the total number of tomato plants in the rows.

   b. What is the slope of the line?

   _____

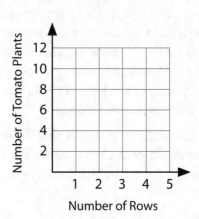

4. Raku is making muffins. For every 1 cup of sugar, there are 3 cups of flour.

   a. Graph the proportional relationship between cups of sugar and cups of flour.

   b. What is the slope of the line?

   _____

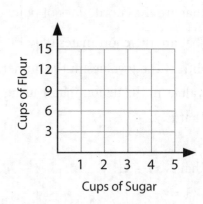

Name: _____ **Date:** _____

Directions: Solve each problem.

1. Maeve is looking for the best deal on strawberries. She looks at two different grocery stores for pricing.

   Which store has the lower price per pound of strawberries?

   _____

Gary's Groceries

Pounds of Strawberries	Cost
3	$6.75
6	$13.50
9	$20.25

Marty's Market

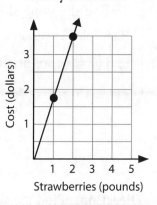

2. Joaquin is pricing dog food at local stores.

   Which store has the lower price per pound of dog food?

   _____

Store A

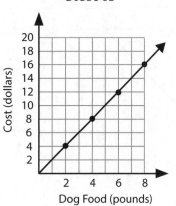

Dog Food (pounds)

Store B

$y = 2.5x$

3. Marco is pricing streaming services.

   Which streaming service has the lower price per movie?

   _____

Streaming Service A

(per movie): $y = 7.5x$

Streaming Service B

Number of Movies	Cost
4	$28
7	$49
10	$70

4. Two different babysitting rates are shown.

   Which babysitter is earning more dollars per hour?

   _____

Babysitter A

Hours	Earnings
3	$42
6	$84
9	$126

Babysitter B

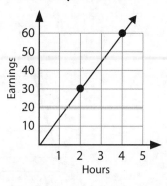

Proportional Relationships and Slope

Name: _____   Date: _____

Example

To find the slope of a line, choose any two points on the line.

Example: Two points on the graph are (3, 2) and (6, 4).

$\frac{4-2}{6-3} = \frac{2}{3}$, so the slope of the line on the graph is $\frac{2}{3}$.

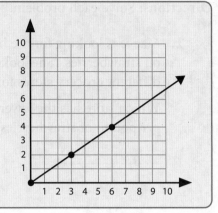

Directions: Find the slope of each line.

1. slope: _____

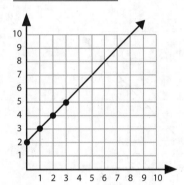

4. slope: _____

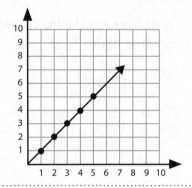

2. slope: _____

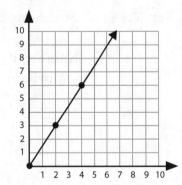

5. slope: _____

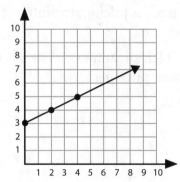

3. slope: _____

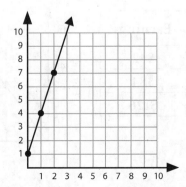

6. slope: _____

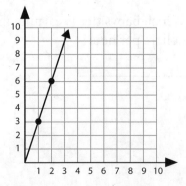

Name: _____ Date: _____

Quick Tip

Equations of proportional relationships are written as $y = mx$, where m is the constant of proportionality, or the slope. Equations that are not proportional are written as $y = mx + b$, where m is the slope and b is the y-intercept.

The equation for this graph is $y = 2x + 1$ because the slope is $\frac{2}{1}$ and the y-intercept is 1.

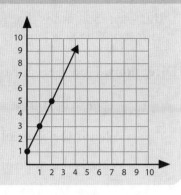

Directions: Write an equation for each line.

1. $y =$ _____

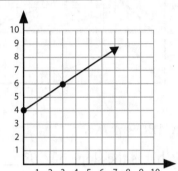

2. $y =$ _____

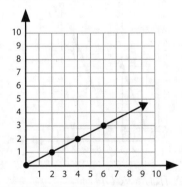

3. $y =$ _____

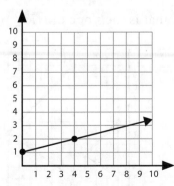

4. $y =$ _____

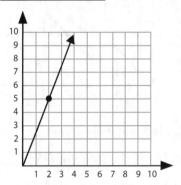

5. $y =$ _____

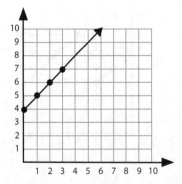

6. $y =$ _____

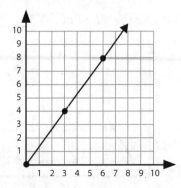

Proportional Relationships and Slope

Name: _____   Date: _____

👉 Quick Tip

The ~ symbol means that two shapes are similar. They are the same shape but have proportional corresponding side lengths.

Directions: Find the slope of the indicated side for each triangle.

1. Δ ABC ~ Δ DEF

What is the slope of $\overline{AB}$? _____

What is the slope of $\overline{DE}$? _____

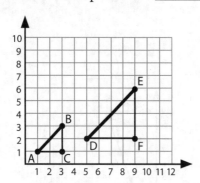

4. Δ ABC ~ Δ XYZ

What is the slope of $\overline{AB}$? _____

What is the slope of $\overline{XY}$? _____

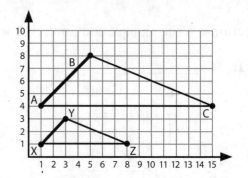

2. Δ QRS ~ Δ TUV

What is the slope of $\overline{QS}$? _____

What is the slope of $\overline{TV}$? _____

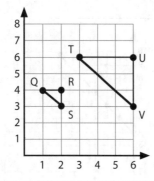

5. Δ ABC ~ Δ JKL

What is the slope of $\overline{AB}$? _____

What is the slope of $\overline{JK}$? _____

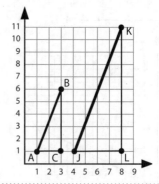

3. Δ MNP ~ Δ XYZ

What is the slope of $\overline{MN}$? _____

What is the slope of $\overline{XY}$? _____

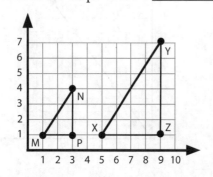

6. Δ JKL ~ Δ GHI

What is the slope of $\overline{KL}$? _____

What is the slope of $\overline{HI}$? _____

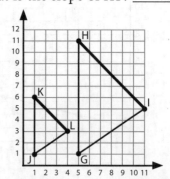

Learn about Linear Equations, Expressions, and Inequalities

A **linear expression** is a mathematical statement made up of terms with constants (fixed values) and/or variables (letters that represents unknown numbers).

A **linear equation** is a mathematical statement between two mathematical expressions that are equal to each other.

To solve linear equations, you can isolate the variable on one side of the equation. Follow these steps when solving equations:

1. Complete the Distributive Property.

2. Combine any like terms on the same side of the equal sign.

3. Complete the inverse of addition or subtraction.

4. Complete the inverse of multiplication or division.

Equations can have one solution, no solution, or infinitely many solutions.

An equation that has **one solution** will result in a variable equal to a number. Example: $x = 4$

An equation that has **no solution** will result in a solution that is a false statement. Example: $8 = 2$

An equation that has **infinitely many** solutions will result in a number or variable equal to itself. Example: $5 = 5$

Example 1

Solve the equation.

$2x + 7 = 23$

1. Do the inverse of adding 7 to both sides of the equation. The inverse of addition is subtraction.

$$\begin{aligned} 2x + 7 &= 23 \\ -7 \quad &-7 \\ 2x &= 16 \end{aligned}$$

2. Next, do the inverse of multiplication, which is division. Divide both sides of the equation by 2.

$$\frac{2x}{2} = \frac{16}{2}$$

$$x = 8$$

Example 2

Solve the inequality, and graph the solution.

$3(x - 5) < 30$

1. Divide both sides of the equation by 3.

$$\frac{3(x - 5)}{3} < \frac{30}{3}$$

$$x - 5 < 10$$

2. Add 5 to each side of the inequality.

$$\begin{aligned} x - 5 &< 10 \\ +5 \quad &+5 \\ x &< 15 \end{aligned}$$

3. Graph the inequality. If the symbol is < or >, the number found should not be included in the solution. It would be an open dot on the number line. If the symbol is ≤ or ≥, the number found is a solution and would be a closed dot on the number line. The solution here is $x < 15$, so there is an open dot on 15. Because the solutions are less than the number, shade the number line to the left of 15.

Learn about Linear Equations, Expressions, and Inequalities *(cont.)*

Example 3

Solve the equation.

$9(x - 3) - 2x + 10 = 4(x - 4)$

1. Complete the Distributive Property on both sides of the equation.

   $9(x - 3) = 9x - 27$

   $4(x - 4) = 4x - 16$

2. Combine like terms.

   $9x - 27 - 2x + 10 = 4x - 16$

   $7x - 17 = 4x - 16$

3. Isolate the variable by subtracting $4x$ from each side of the equation.

   $3x - 17 = -16$

4. Add 17 to each side of the equation.

   $3x = 1$

5. Divide each side of the equation by 3.

   $x = \frac{1}{3}$

Example 4

Jeff is buying 4 pots for his garden and a $12 tomato plant. He spent $76.

How much was each pot? Write and solve an equation to represent the problem.

1. You do not know the price of each pot, but you know Jeff is buying 4 of them, so you can write $4x$ to represent the cost of the pots.

2. You know that Jeff also spent $12 on the tomato plant, for a total of $76. So, you can add $4x$ and 12. The equation looks like this:

   $4x + 12 = 76$

3. Solve the equation. Subtract 12 from both sides of the equation, and then divide both sides by 4.

   $4x + 12 = 76$

   $-12 \quad -12$ subtract 12

   $\dfrac{4x}{4} = \dfrac{64}{4}$ divide by 4

   $x = 16$

4. What is the price of each pot? _____

80 142250—180 Days of Math © Shell Education

Name: _____ **Date:** _____

Directions: Solve each equation. Show your work.

1. $3x + 6 = 39$

$x = $ _____

2. $4(x - 8) = 40$

$x = $ _____

3. $-9x - 5 = 22$

$x = $ _____

4. $8x + 12 = 20$

$x = $ _____

5. $6(x - 7) = 36$

$x = $ _____

6. $5x - 6 = 39$

$x = $ _____

7. $3(x - 4) = 45$

$x = $ _____

8. $2(x + 9) = -50$

$x = $ _____

9. $7(x + 2) = 63$

$x = $ _____

10. $10x - 5 = 25$

$x = $ _____

11. $2x - 9 = 13$

$x = $ _____

12. $9(x + 1) = -72$

$x = $ _____

13. $-4(x - 8) = 36$

$x = $ _____

14. $-3x + 11 = 44$

$x = $ _____

Linear Equations, Expressions, and Inequalities

Name: _____ **Date:** _____

✎ Quick Tip

Equations with one solution have x equal to a number. Equations with no solution end with a false statement, and equations with an infinite number of solutions have a number or variable equal to itself.

Directions: Solve each equation. Then, circle whether it has one solution, no solution, or infinite solutions.

1. $4(x + 6) = 3(x + 8) + x$

   a. $x =$ _____

   b. one solution

       no solution

       infinite solutions

6. $3x - 4(2 - x) = 7(x - 4)$

   a. $x =$ _____

   b. one solution

       no solution

       infinite solutions

2. $9x - 10 = 4(x + 3) + 5x$

   a. $x =$ _____

   b. one solution

       no solution

       infinite solutions

7. $-2(x + 5) - 3x = -2(2x + 7)$

   a. $x =$ _____

   b. one solution

       no solution

       infinite solutions

3. $8(x - 6) + 4x = 2(4x - 12)$

   a. $x =$ _____

   b. one solution

       no solution

       infinite solutions

8. $-4(x - 3) = 2(6 - 2x)$

   a. $x =$ _____

   b. one solution

       no solution

       infinite solutions

4. $6(x - 3) + 9 = 2(3x - 7)$

   a. $x =$ _____

   b. one solution

       no solution

       infinite solutions

9. $7(3x - 2) + 3x - 1 = 3(8x - 5)$

   a. $x =$ _____

   b. one solution

       no solution

       infinite solutions

5. $3(x - 2) + 5x = 2(4 - x)$

   a. $x =$ _____

   b. one solution

       no solution

       infinite solutions

10. $10(x - 4) = 2(x + 4)$

   a. $x =$ _____

   b. one solution

       no solution

       infinite solutions

Directions: Solve each equation. Show your work.

1. $3(2x + 4) = 2(x - 4)$

$x =$ _____

2. $\frac{3}{4}(8x - 12) = 5(x - 1)$

$x =$ _____

3. $6x + 8(x - \frac{3}{8}) = 4x - 2(x - \frac{1}{2})$

$x =$ _____

4. $\frac{1}{2}x + 4 - 3(2 + x) = 2(\frac{3}{4}x + 1)$

$x =$ _____

5. $\frac{9}{5}(10x - 10) + 2x = 4(x - 5)$

$x =$ _____

6. $\frac{3}{2}x + 7 + 2(\frac{1}{2}x - \frac{1}{2}) = 0.5x + 6$

$x =$ _____

7. $\frac{4}{5}(25x - 15) = \frac{3}{5}(10x - 20) + 28$

$x =$ _____

8. $1.5x - 2(3.5x - 4) = 3(4.5x - 10)$

$x =$ _____

9. $2.8x - 4(3.1x + 4) = 22.4$

$x =$ _____

10. $8(x - 3) + 2(x + 4) = 3(x + 1) + 4(x + 2)$

$x =$ _____

Linear Equations, Expressions, and Inequalities

Name: _____ **Date:** _____

> ### ✎ Quick Tip
> open dot: < less than; > greater than
> closed dot: ≤ less than or equal to; ≥ greater than or equal to

Directions: Solve each inequality, and graph the solution on the number line.

1. $2(x - 7) < 10$ **a.** _____

     b.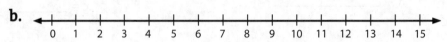

2. $5(x + 1) \geq 25$ **a.** _____

     b.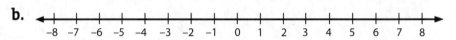

3. $4(x - 6) + 2x > 12$ **a.** _____

     b.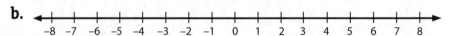

4. $8x + 11 \leq 51$ **a.** _____

     b.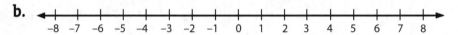

5. $9x + x - 8 > 32$ **a.** _____

     b.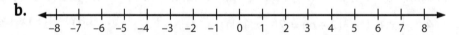

6. $5(x - 3) < 15$ **a.** _____

     b.

7. $3(x + 2) + 3x \geq 24$ **a.** _____

     b.

8. $2(x + 4) \geq 14$ **a.** _____

     b.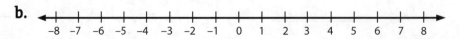

Name: _____ Date: _____

Directions: Write and solve an equation or inequality to represent each problem.

1. Mya is painting a fence. She has already painted 30 feet of the fence and has to paint equal parts of the remaining fence for 3 more days. When she is finished, she will have all 120 feet painted. How many feet does Mya need to paint each of the 3 days?

   a. Equation: _____

   b. Solution: _____

2. Harriet is shopping for supplies for the art club. She has to buy 4 packages of posterboard, a bottle of paint for $4, and a package of paintbrushes for $8. She can spend no more than $48. How much can each package of posterboard cost?

   a. Inequality: _____

   b. Solution: _____

3. Armond and 3 of his friends went to dinner. They each had a sandwich and a $2 order of french fries. The total bill was $56. How much did each sandwich cost?

   a. Equation: _____

   b. Solution: _____

4. Li is shopping for a gift for his sister. He bought 3 video games and a $26 volleyball. Li has $182 to spend. How much does each video game cost?

   a. Inequality: _____

   b. Solution: _____

5. Margo bought 5 sweaters and a $40 pair of jeans. She spent $320. How much was each sweater?

   a. Equation: _____

   b. Solution: _____

6. Juan purchased 7 bottles of sports drink and a $7 bag of potato chips for his friends. Juan spent $35. What did each bottle of sports drink cost?

   a. Equation: _____

   b. Solution: _____

7. Pierre and his parents went to dinner. Pierre was able to pay for the meal with a $60 gift card. Each of them had an entrée and an additional $6 side dish. What did each entrée cost?

   a. Inequality: _____

   b. Solution: _____

8. Sean is buying groceries. He bought 3 packages of cookies, an $18 steak, and $3 of potatoes. Sean spent $48. How much did Sean pay for each package of cookies?

   a. Equation: _____

   b. Solution: _____

Learn about Simultaneous Equations

A **system of linear equations** (or simultaneous equations) is a group of two or more linear equations.

A **solution** to a system of equations can be one of three possibilities.

1. one solution—the point at which the lines intersect

2. no solution—the lines are parallel and therefore do not ever intersect

3. infinite solutions—the lines have the same equation and therefore intersect at every point

Systems of equations can be solved algebraically or graphically. To solve algebraically, solve one of the equations for either x or y. Then, substitute that value into the other equation to solve for the other variable. To solve graphically, graph both equations, and find if or where they intersect.

Check a Solution

Is $(-5, -2)$ a solution to the system of linear equations?

$$y = \frac{2}{5x}$$
$$y = -x - 7$$

1. Substitute -5 for x and -2 for y into the first equation and solve. If the equation is a true statement, the given point is a solution.

   $$-2 = \frac{2}{5}(-5)$$
   $$-2 = \frac{-10}{5}$$
   $$-2 = -2$$

   Since -2 is equal to itself, the point is a solution for this equation.

2. Substitute -5 for x and -2 for y into the second equation and solve. If the equation is a true statement, the given point is a solution.

   $$-2 = -(-5) - 7$$
   $$-2 = 5 - 7$$
   $$-2 = -2$$

   Since -2 is equal to itself, the point is a solution for this equation.

3. Since the point $(-5, -2)$ is a solution to both equations, then it is a solution for the system of equations.

Learn about Simultaneous Equations *(cont.)*

Solve Algebraically

$3x + y = 4$

$x - y = 8$

1. Solve the first equation for y.

$y = -3x + 4$

2. Substitute $-3x + 4$ into the second equation for y, and solve for x.

$x - (-3x + 4) = 8$

$x + 3x - 4 = 8$

$4x - 4 = 8$

$4x = 12$

$x = 3$

3. Substitute the solution from step 2 into the first equation for x. Solve the equation for y.

$3(3) + y = 4$

$9 + y = 4$

$y = -5$

4. The solution to the system of equations is $(3, -5)$.

Solve Graphically

Identify whether there is no solution, infinitely many solutions, or one solution. If there is one solution, write the coordinates of the point.

$y = 2x + 2$

$y = -2x + 6$

1. Graph each line on the same coordinate plane.

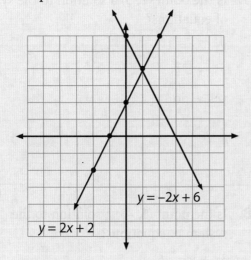

$y = 2x + 2$

$y = -2x + 6$

2. Do the lines intersect? _____

3. What are the coordinates of the point where the lines intersect? _____

The point of intersection is the solution to the system of linear equations.

Name: _____   Date: _____

Directions: Determine whether each given point is a solution to the system of equations. Circle *yes* or *no*.

1. Is the point (0, 3) a solution to the system of equations?

$y = x + 2$

$y = -2x + 2$

yes   no

2. Is the point (–3, 1) a solution to the system of equations?

$x + y = -2$

$y = \frac{1}{3}x + 2$

yes   no

3. Is the point (0, –3) a solution to the system of equations?

$y - \frac{3}{2}x = -3$

$y + 3 = -3x$

yes   no

4. Is the point (4, –2) a solution to the system of equations?

$4 + y = \frac{2}{3x}$

$y = \frac{-1}{3x} - 1$

yes   no

5. Is the point (–1, 1) a solution to the system of equations?

$2x + y = -1$

$y - 2x = 3$

yes   no

6. Is the point (1, –3) a solution to the system of equations?

$3x + y = 3$

$y - 2x = -4$

yes   no

7. Is the point (2, 5) a solution to the system of equations?

$y - 2x = 1$

$y + x = 7$

yes   no

8. Is the point (1, –3) a solution to the system of equations?

$3x + y = -6$

$y - 2x = -1$

yes   no

✏️ **Reminder**

To graph a linear equation, write the equation in slope-intercept form: $y = mx + b$. Plot the y-intercept on the y-axis. From the y-intercept, count the slope (rise/run), and plot the second point. Connect the points to form the line.

Directions: Solve each system of equations by graphing. Write the solution to each system.

1. $y = \frac{3}{2}x - 2$

   $x + y = 4$

   a.

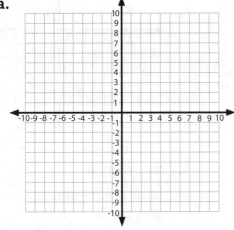

   b. Solution: _____

3. $y = -x$

   $y - 5 = \frac{2}{3x}$

   a.

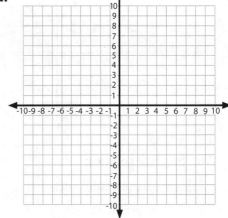

   b. Solution: _____

2. $2x + y = -1$

   $y - 3x = -1$

   a.

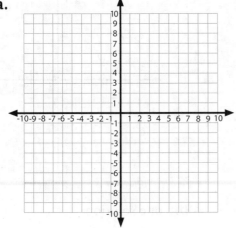

   b. Solution: _____

4. $2x + y = 9$

   $y = 2x + 1$

   a.

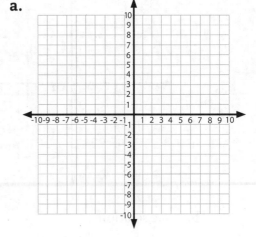

   b. Solution: _____

Simultaneous Equations

Name: _____ Date: _____

Directions: Graph each system of equations to find the solution. Then, circle whether the system has one solution, infinite solutions, or no solution. If there is one solution, write the coordinates of the point.

1. $y - x = 1$

$y - 5 = -x$

a.
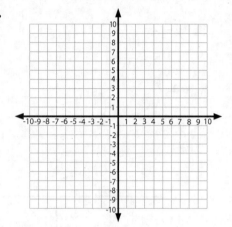

b. one solution

infinite solutions

no solution

3. $y = -4x$

$-28x = 7y$

a.
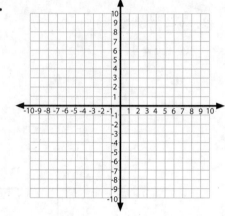

b. one solution

infinite solutions

no solution

2. $\frac{-1}{3}x + y = -1$

$2x + y = -1$

a.
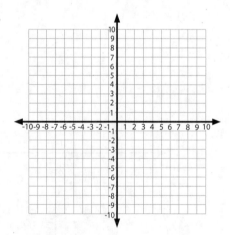

b. one solution

infinite solutions

no solution

4. $-3x + y = 6$

$3x - y = 13$

a.
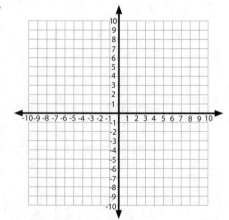

b. one solution

infinite solutions

no solution

Name: _____ Date: _____

📝 Reminder

Solve one equation for x or y. Substitute the expression into the other equation, and solve it. Write the solution as an ordered pair.

Directions: Solve each system of equations algebraically. Write the solution on the line.

1. $y + x = 4$
$2x + y = 12$

Solution: _____

2. $3x - y = 8$
$4x + y = 20$

Solution: _____

3. $6x - 3y = 18$
$2y + 3x = 30$

Solution: _____

4. $x - 8y = 40$
$3x + y = 70$

Solution: _____

5. $x + 3y = 9$
$4x + y = 14$

Solution: _____

6. $9x + 8y = 55$
$3x + y = 20$

Solution: _____

7. $4x + y = 18$
$x + y = 30$

Solution: _____

8. $y = 3x$
$4x + y = 56$

Solution: _____

Simultaneous Equations

Name: _____ Date: _____

Directions: Graph each system of equations to find the solution.

1. $y - 3x = 8$

$y = -x$

a.

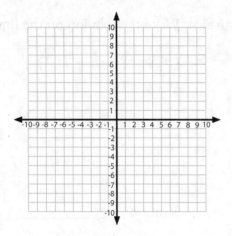

b. Solution: _____

2. $y = 5x + 3$

$3y - 15x = 9$

a.

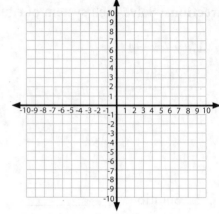

b. Solution: _____

Directions: Circle whether each given point is a solution to the systems of equations.

3. $y = \frac{1}{3}x$

$y - x = -4$

Is (3, –1) a solution?

yes   no

4. $y = 2x$

$3x + y = 10$

Is (–2, 4) a solution?

yes   no

Directions: Circle how many solutions the systems of equations have.

5. $y = 4x + 6$

$-8x + 2y = 16$

one solution

no solution

infinite solutions

6. $6x + 3y = 18$

$2x + y = 6$

one solution

no solution

infinite solutions

Simultaneous Equations

Directions: Solve each problem. Use a calculator when asked for decimal approximations of square roots.

1. Reba is researching monthly gym memberships to find the lower price. Which gym has the lower price per month?

Gym A: $y = 19.25x$

Gym B:

Number of Months	Price per Month
2	$37
4	$74
6	$111

_____

2. $12^3 =$ _____

3. $(2.3 \times 10^2) + (4.5 \times 10^2) =$

_____

4. Write 31 as a ratio.

_____

5. Write a decimal approximation for $\sqrt{13}$ rounded to the nearest hundredth.

_____

6. $3[2 + (5 - 7)^2] + 3(-2) =$ _____

7. Write $0.\overline{4}$ as a fraction.

_____

8. Plot the numbers on the number line.
$\sqrt{101}, \sqrt{120}, \sqrt{115}$

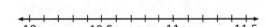

9. Answer the questions.

  a. Which two consecutive integers is $\sqrt{116}$ between?

  _____ and _____

  b. Which integer is $\sqrt{116}$ closer to?

  _____

  c. What is the decimal approximation for $\sqrt{116}$ rounded to the nearest hundredth?

  _____

10. $8(x - 9) + 2x = 100$

  $x =$ _____

Spiral Review

Name: _____ **Date:** _____

Spiral Review

Directions: Solve each problem.

1. Solve the system of equations algebraically.

$y - 5 = \frac{3}{2}x$

$y = -x$

Solution: _____

2. Match each number with the location on the number line.

$\sqrt{88}, 9\frac{1}{5}, \sqrt{75}$

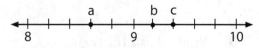

a. _____

b. _____

c. _____

3. $2(x - 4) + (-4x) + 7 = 3(x - 5)$

$x =$ _____

4. Does the graph show a proportional relationship?

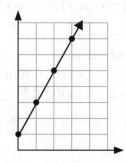

_____

5. $(2.3 \times 10^8)(1.6 \times 10^2) =$ _____

6. Write $\frac{14}{3}$ as a decimal.

_____

7. Circle the larger number.

$\sqrt[3]{64}$ or $4\frac{1}{4}$

8. Solve the inequality, and graph it on the number line.

$3x - 8 < 16$

a. Solution: _____

b.

Spiral Review

Directions: Solve each problem.

1. $\dfrac{(8.4 \times 10^5)}{(2.1 \times 10^3)} =$ _____

5. $4^3 - 8^2 =$ _____

2. Is $(6, -1)$ a solution to the system of equations?

$x - 4y = 10$

$2x - 2y = 14$

_____

6. Write $\dfrac{95}{4}$ as a decimal.

_____

3. Michael recorded the number of batches of cookies he baked after school each day this week.

Day	Batches of Cookies
1	6.5
2	13
3	19.5
4	26
5	32.5

a. Graph Michaels's cookie baking data.

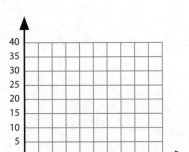

b. Is the relationship between day and number of batches proportional?

_____

c. What is the slope of the line?

_____

7. $(7.4 \times 10^4) - (4.1 \times 10^4) =$ _____

8. Does the graph represent a proportional relationship?

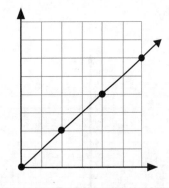

_____

9. $4(3x + 1) - 10x = 34$

$x =$ _____

4. $\sqrt[3]{343} =$ _____

10. $9^2 - \sqrt{64} =$ _____

Name: _____ Date: _____

Directions: Solve each problem. Use a calculator when asked for decimal approximations of square roots.

1. Match each number with a location on the number line.

$3\frac{5}{9}$, $\sqrt{15}$, 3.25

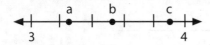

  a. _____

  b. _____

  c. _____

2. $(2.8 \times 10^3)(1.6 \times 10^5) = $ _____

3. Solve the system of equations by graphing.

$x + 1 = y$

$3x - y = 1$

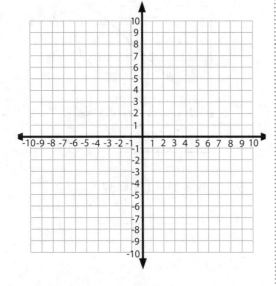

Solution: _____

4. What is the decimal approximation of $\sqrt{8}$ rounded to the nearest tenth?

_____

5. Write 76,000,000 in scientific notation.

_____

6. $x^2 = 144$

$x = $ _____

7. $\sqrt{n^2} = $ _____

8. Plot the approximate value of $\sqrt{31}$ on the number line.

9. $\frac{1}{4}(8 - 12) + 32 + \sqrt{(62 + 82)} = $ _____

10. Write 5.7×10^{-1} in standard form.

_____

Directions: Solve each problem. Use a calculator when asked for decimal approximations of square roots.

1. Solve the system of equations algebraically.

$y + 4x = 16$

$2x + y = 34$

Solution: _____

2. Which pizza shop has the lower price per pizza?

Paulie's Pizzeria: $y = 8.25x$

Pizza Palace:

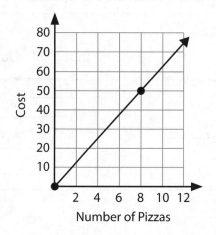

_____

3. Plot the decimal approximation rounded to the nearest tenth.

$5 + \sqrt{33}$

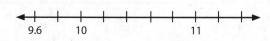

4. $13^2 =$ _____

5. $\triangle ABC \sim \triangle FGH$

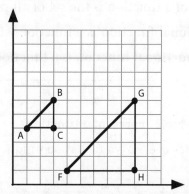

a. What is the slope of line AB?

_____

b. What is the slope of line FG?

_____

6. $(2.7 \times 10^3) + (1.6 \times 10^2) =$ _____

7. $(\frac{1}{2})^3 \times 24 + 2^2 - 3(9 - 10) =$ _____

8. $x^3 = 512$

$x =$ _____

Spiral Review

Learn about Functions

A **function** is a rule that results in exactly one unique output for each input.

The **domain** of a function is the set of all numbers that are put into a function, or the *x*-values.

The **range** of a function is the set of all numbers that come out of a function, or the *y*-values.

A **proportional** function is a function where the output is equal to the input times a constant.

A **nonproportional** function is a function where the ratio of output to input is not constant.

Example 1

Does the table represent a function?

1. Does every *x*-value have a unique *y*-value?

   _____

2. Since every *x*-value has a unique *y*-value, the relationship represented in the table is a function.

x	y
1	4
2	5
3	6
4	7

Example 2

Does the mapping diagram represent a function?

1. Does each input value have only one unique output value?

   _____

2. Since every input does not have a unique output value, the relationship is not a function.

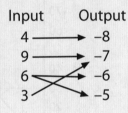

Input	Output
4	−8
9	−7
6	−6
3	−5

Example 3

Does the graph represent a function?

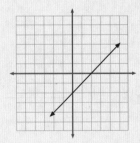

1. Draw a vertical line anywhere on the graph. The vertical line should only intersect the graph at one point, regardless of where the line is drawn. If the vertical line crosses the graph at more than one location, the graph is not a function.

2. Does each vertical line intersect the graph at only one point?

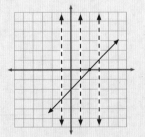

   _____

3. Since the vertical lines each intersect the graph at only one point, the graph is a function.

Learn about Functions *(cont.)*

Example 4

Find the range of values for the domain of the function.

$y = 3x + 1$

Domain: 0, 1, 2, 3

1. To find the range, substitute each number from the domain into the function. The solutions are the range.

2. If $x = 0$, $y =$ _____

   If $x = 1$, $y =$ _____

   If $x = 2$, $y =$ _____

   If $x = 3$, $y =$ _____

3. The range is made up of the outputs when putting the given numbers for the domain in as the inputs. So, the range is 1, 4, 7, 10.

Example 5

Is the function represented in the table a proportional relationship?

Input	Output
0	0
1	2
2	4
3	6

1. For a relationship to be proportional, the ratio of input to output should be a constant. You can multiply each input value by the same number to get output.

   $2 \div 1 =$ _____

   $4 \div 2 =$ _____

   $6 \div 3 =$ _____

2. Since the answer is the same for each ratio, the relationship is proportional.

Name: _____   **Date:** _____

Directions: Circle whether each table, map, or graph represents a function. If it is not a function, explain why.

1. yes   no

_____

x	y
6	–3
12	2
8	–8
7	6
–4	–3

4. yes   no

_____

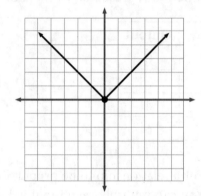

2. yes   no

_____

x	y
–3	15
–4	9
–5	6
–6	4
–7	–7

5. yes   no

_____

3. yes   no

_____

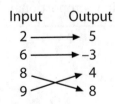

6. yes   no

_____

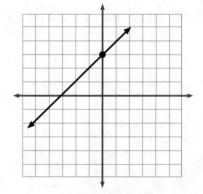

Name: _____   Date: _____

Directions: Write the range of each function when given the domain.

1. $y = 4x$

Domain: 2, 5, 7, 10

Range: _____

2. $y = x - 6$

Domain: –2, –4, –6, –8

Range: _____

3. $y = -x$

Domain: –3, 5, 9, 11

Range: _____

4. $y = -2x$

Domain: –3, 7, –8, 10

Range: _____

5. $y = \frac{x}{2}$

Domain: –4, –2, 2, 4

Range: _____

6. $y = \frac{-2x}{3}$

Domain: –6, –3, 3, 6

Range: _____

Directions: Circle whether each relationship is proportional or nonproportional.

7. proportional   nonproportional

Input	Output
0	3
2	7
4	11
6	15

8. proportional   nonproportional

Input	Output
1	2
2	5
3	8
4	11
5	14

9. proportional   nonproportional

Input	Output
10	40
20	80
30	120
40	160
50	200

10. proportional   nonproportional

Input	Output
5	15
10	30
15	45
20	60
25	75

11. proportional   nonproportional

Input	Output
2	–16
4	–32
6	–48
8	–64
10	–80

12. proportional   nonproportional

Input	Output
6	8
12	14
18	20
24	26
30	32

Functions

Name: _____ Date: _____

📝 Reminder

Linear equations are written in the form $y = mx + b$, where m is the slope and b is the y-intercept. The y-intercept is the point where the graph crosses the y-axis.

To find the slope of a line, choose two points and subtract: $\dfrac{y_2 - y_1}{x_2 - x_1}$

Directions: Answer the questions.

1. Which function has a greater slope?

_____

Function A

x	y
1	5
2	9
3	13
4	17

Function B

4. Which function has a smaller y-intercept?

_____

Function A:
$y = -4x - 6$

Function B:

x	y
-2	-1
0	-5
2	-9
4	-13

2. Which function has a greater slope?

_____

Function A

x	y
2	-5
3	-8
4	-11
5	-14

Function B

5. Which function has a smaller slope?

_____

Function A:
$y = \frac{1}{2}x$

Function B:

x	y
4	1
2	$\frac{1}{2}$
0	0
-2	$\frac{-1}{2}$

3. Which function has a greater y-intercept?

_____

Function A

x	y
-1	-3
0	-2
1	-1

Function B

6. Which function has a greater y-intercept?

_____

Function A:
$y = 9x + 1$

Function B:

x	y
-3	-13
-2	-10
-1	-7
0	-4

 142250—180 Days of Math

👆 Quick Tip

Slope is the rate of change for a function. The higher the slope, the faster the rate of change.

Directions: Answer the questions.

1. Which function is increasing at a faster rate?

_____

Function A		Function B

x	y
–4	–1
0	0
4	1
8	2

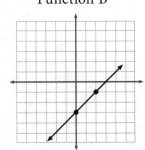

2. Which function is increasing at a slower rate?

_____

Function A   Function B

x	y
–1	3
0	5
1	7
2	9

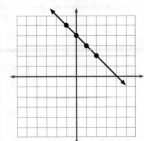

3. Which function has a smaller y-intercept?

_____

Function A   Function B

x	y
–1	2
0	3
1	4
2	5

4. Which function has a greater y-intercept?

_____

Function A   Function B:
$y = -4x - 6$

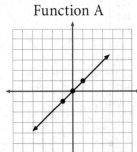

5. Which function has a smaller slope?

_____

Function A   Function B:
$y = 3x$

6. Which function has a greater rate of increase?

_____

Function A   Function B:
$y = \frac{3}{5}x + 2$

Functions

Name: _____ **Date:** _____

Directions: Solve each problem.

1. Rodrigo is looking for the best price on his cell phone plan. Plan A charges $3 per minute plus a $50 monthly fee. Plan B is represented by the function $y = 4x + 25$. Which plan should Rodrigo choose if he wants the lower cost of price *per minute*?

_____

2. Maurico wants to buy a car that gets the greatest number of miles per gallon. He researches and finds that car A gets 22 miles per gallon. Car B's mileage is represented by the graph. Which car will give Maurico the most miles per gallon?

_____

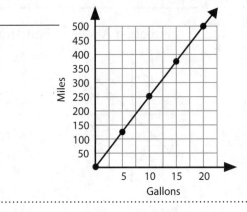
Miles / Gallons

3. Marla needs new tires for her car. She checks the cost at two different shops. Which shop offers the lower price per tire?

_____

Terri's Tires

Number of Tires	Cost
1	$90
2	$180
3	$270
4	$360

Willie's Wheels

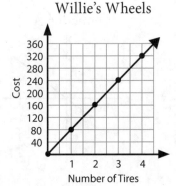
Cost / Number of Tires

4. Kaia earns $15 per hour babysitting. Mackenzie works at Burger Barn, and her pay rate is represented on the graph. Who earns more money per hour?

_____

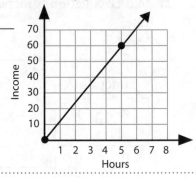
Income / Hours

5. Ryan wants to join a gym. Gym A offered him a plan represented by the equation $y = 12x + 50$. Gym B offered him the plan represented by the table. Which gym offers a lower initial fee?

_____

Number of Months	Cost
0	$75
1	$95
2	$115
3	$135
4	$155

6. Sudo spent $y = 5x + 15$ to rent a boat at the dock. Gio rented a jet ski at the dock, and his cost is represented on the graph. Who paid more per hour for their rental?

_____

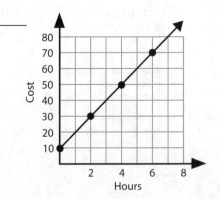
Cost / Hours

Learn about Linear and Nonlinear Functions

A **linear function** has a constant rate of change and can be written in the form $y = mx + b$. The graph of a linear function is a straight line.

An example of a **nonlinear function** is one that has an exponent of a variable greater than 1. The graph of a nonlinear function does not form a straight line.

Example 1

Does the table represent a linear function?

1. Find the rate of change. What operation can be done to each x-term to find the y-term? _____

2. What is the slope of the line? _____

3. Write the equation in $y = mx + b$ form.

   $y =$ _____

x	y
1	4
2	8
3	12
4	16

Example 2

Does the graph represent a linear function?

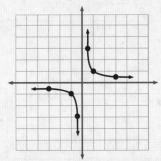

1. Is the graph a straight line? _____

2. If the graph is a straight line, then it is a linear function. If not, it is a nonlinear function. Does the graph represent a linear function? _____

Example 3

Does the equation represent a linear or nonlinear relationship?

$y = x^2$

1. Is the equation in the form $y = mx + b$? _____

   a. If the variable has an exponent greater than 1, it is a nonlinear function. Does the variable have an exponent greater than 1? _____

   b. Does the equation represent a linear or nonlinear function? _____

Name: _____   Date: _____

Directions: Circle whether each table represents a linear or nonlinear function.

1. linear   nonlinear

x	y
−1	6
0	2
1	−2
2	−6

2. linear   nonlinear

x	y
−1	4
0	0
1	3
2	4

3. linear   nonlinear

x	y
2	6
4	8
6	10
8	12

4. linear   nonlinear

x	y
−2	0
0	1
2	2
4	3

5. linear   nonlinear

x	y
3	9
6	18
9	36
12	48

6. linear   nonlinear

x	y
−2	0
−1	2
0	4
1	6

7. linear   nonlinear

x	y
2	6
4	9
6	12
8	15

8. linear   nonlinear

x	y
4	−14
3	−11
2	−8
1	−5

Quick Tip

A graph must be a straight line to represent a linear function.

Directions: Circle whether each graph represents a linear or nonlinear function.

1. linear   nonlinear

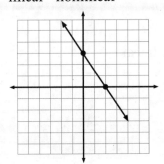

2. linear   nonlinear

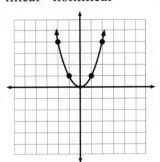

3. linear   nonlinear

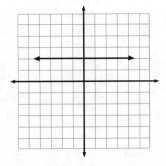

4. linear   nonlinear

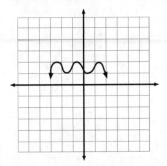

5. linear   nonlinear

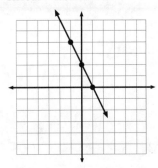

6. linear   nonlinear

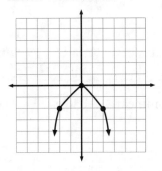

7. linear   nonlinear

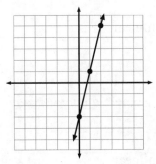

8. linear   nonlinear

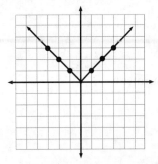

Name: _____ Date: _____

✎ Quick Tip

All linear functions can be written in the form $y = mx + b$, where m is the slope and b is the y-intercept. In this equation, b can be 0. If you're unsure, try to graph the equation.

Directions: Circle whether each equation represents a linear or nonlinear function.

1. $y = 4x^2$

   linear   nonlinear

2. $y = \frac{1}{2}x + 3$

   linear   nonlinear

3. $y = |x|$

   linear   nonlinear

4. $y = 3x$

   linear   nonlinear

5. $y = \frac{2}{x}$

   linear   nonlinear

6. $y = x - 4$

   linear   nonlinear

7. $y = \frac{x}{3} + 1$

   linear   nonlinear

8. $y = x^2 - 1$

   linear   nonlinear

9. $y = x^3$

   linear   nonlinear

10. $y = -x$

   linear   nonlinear

11. $y = 5x + 9$

   linear   nonlinear

12. $y = -\frac{2}{3}x$

   linear   nonlinear

Name: _____ Date: _____

Directions: Circle whether each table represents a linear or nonlinear function.

1.

Input	Output
7	21
8	24
9	27

linear   nonlinear

2.

Input	Output
4	6
5	8
6	10

linear   nonlinear

3.

Input	Output
–2	–14
–1	–7
0	0
1	7

linear   nonlinear

4.

Input	Output
–4	8
–2	4
0	0

linear   nonlinear

5.

Input	Output
–9	–45
–8	–48
–7	–35
–6	–36

linear   nonlinear

6.

Input	Output
20	–20
30	–36
40	–40

linear   nonlinear

7.

Input	Output
11	22
12	36
13	52

linear   nonlinear

8.

Input	Output
2	10
3	15
4	20

linear   nonlinear

Name: _____   Date: _____

Directions: Circle whether each relationship represents a linear or nonlinear function.

1.

Input	Output
12	36
14	42
16	48

linear   nonlinear

5.

Input	Output
–2	8
–1	4
0	0
1	–4

linear   nonlinear

2. $y = 7x + 1$

linear   nonlinear

6. $y = -3x^2 + 3$

linear   nonlinear

3.

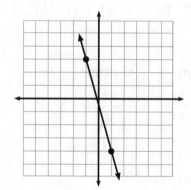

linear   nonlinear

7.

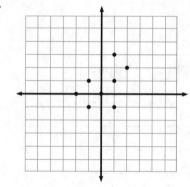

linear   nonlinear

4.

x	y
–6	–12
–5	–10
–4	–8

linear   nonlinear

8. $y = 6x$

linear   nonlinear

Linear and Nonlinear Functions

Learn about Rate of Change

The **rate of change** in a linear function is the slope of the function. In an equation, the rate of change is the coefficient of x. If you know two points on the linear function, you can find the slope, or rate of change, by subtracting:

$$\frac{y_2 - y_1}{x_2 - x_1}$$

For example, if the points (4, 5) and (2, 3) are on the graph of the function, you can subtract to find the slope.

$$\frac{(5-3)}{(4-2)} = \frac{2}{2} = 1$$

So, the rate of change for the linear function is 1.

Example 1

Write an equation to model the function in the table.

x	0	1	2	3
y	2	3	4	5

1. First, you can find the rate of change from the table. Choose two points. You can use (0, 2) and (1, 3). Subtract $\frac{y_2 - y_1}{x_2 - x_1}$.

   $$\frac{(3-2)}{(1-0)} = \frac{1}{1} = 1$$

2. Looking at the table and knowing the slope, you can determine what is the y-intercept is. The y-intercept is where $y = 0$. So, if we imagine columns to the left of the first one, you would get (–1, 1), then (–2, 0). The y-intercept is at –2.

3. Write the equation for the function in $y = mx + b$ form.
   $y = 1x + (–2)$
   Simplify this further to get $y = x - 2$

Example 2

Write an equation to model the function shown on the graph.

1. Find the rate of change from the graph. Choose two points on the graph to calculate the rate of change. You can use (1, 0) and (0, 2). Subtract.

   $$\frac{(2-0)}{(0-1)} = \frac{2}{-1} = -2$$

2. The y-intercept for this graph is 2.

3. Write the equation.

   $y = -2x + 2$

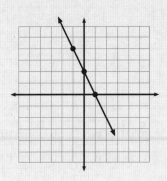

Name: _____   Date: _____

✎ Quick Tip
Remember to write the equations in $y = mx + b$ form.

Directions: Write an equation to model the function in each table.

1.

x	–1	0	1	2
y	–1	1	3	5

$y =$ _____

2.

x	–2	0	2	4
y	–14	–4	6	16

$y =$ _____

3.

x	1	2	3	4
y	5	10	15	20

$y =$ _____

4.

x	10	20	30	40
y	2	4	6	8

$y =$ _____

5.

x	5	10	15	20
y	0	10	20	30

$y =$ _____

6.

x	0	1	2	3
y	2	3	4	5

$y =$ _____

7.

x	2	4	6	8
y	1	2	3	4

$y =$ _____

8.

x	15	20	25	30
y	8	13	18	23

$y =$ _____

9.

x	–4	–2	0	2
y	–20	–10	0	10

$y =$ _____

10.

x	–2	–1	0	1
y	–4	–1	2	5

$y =$ _____

Name: _____   Date: _____

Directions: Each graph shows a linear function. Answer the questions.

1.

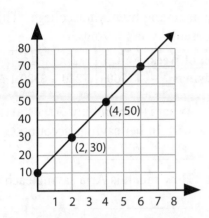

   a. What is the rate of change? _____

   b. What is the initial value? _____

2.

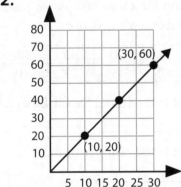

   a. What is the rate of change? _____

   b. What is the initial value? _____

3.

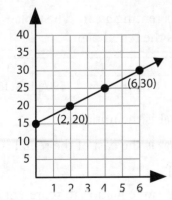

   a. What is the rate of change? _____

   b. What is the initial value? _____

4.

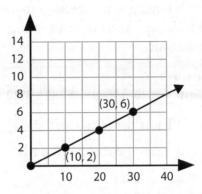

   a. What is the rate of change? _____

   b. What is the initial value? _____

5.

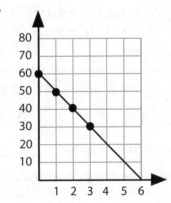

   a. What is the rate of change? _____

   b. What is the initial value? _____

6.

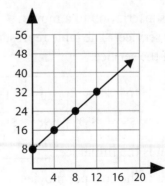

   a. What is the rate of change? _____

   b. What is the initial value? _____

Rate of Change

Name: _____   Date: _____

Directions: Solve each problem.

1. Mary is buying a membership to a gym. The table represents the cost of the membership.

Month	0	1	2	3
Cost	$20	$60	$100	$140

   a. What is the initial fee? _____

   b. What is the cost per month? _____

   c. Write an equation to represent the function.

   $y =$ _____

2. Hank's school is buying sweatshirts for a fundraiser. The table represents the cost of the sweatshirts.

Number of Sweatshirts	0	10	20	30
Cost	$40	$190	$340	$490

   a. What is the initial fee? _____

   b. What is the cost per sweatshirt? _____

   c. Write an equation to represent the function.

   $y =$ _____

3. Eva has a subscription to a movie streaming service. The table represents the cost of the service.

Number of Movies	0	5	10	15
Cost	$8	$53	$98	$143

   a. What is the initial fee? _____

   b. What is the cost per movie? _____

   c. Write an equation to represent the function.

   $y =$ _____

4. Aria is saving money for college. The table represents Aria's savings.

Number of Weeks	0	2	4	6
Savings	$60	$220	$380	$540

   a. What is the amount Aria started with in her savings account? _____

   b. How much is Aria saving each week? _____

   c. Write an equation to represent the function.

   $y =$ _____

5. Bo signed up for a new cell phone plan. The table represents Bo's plan.

Minutes	0	20	40	60
Cost	$75	$155	$235	$315

   a. What is the initial fee for Bo's plan? _____

   b. What is the cost per minute? _____

   c. Write an equation to represent the phone plan.

   $y =$ _____

6. Lorenzo is renting a car. The table represents the rental plan.

Days	0	1	2	3
Cost	$40	$65	$90	$115

   a. What is the initial fee? _____

   b. What is the cost of the rental per day? _____

   c. Write an equation to represent the car rental plan.

   $y =$ _____

Name: _____   **Date:** _____

Directions: Solve each problem.

1. Luis is saving his money. The graph represents Luis's savings plan.

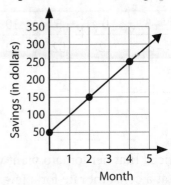

    a. How much money did Luis open his account with? _____

    b. How much money is Luis saving each month? _____

    c. Write an equation to represent Luis's savings plan.

        $y =$ _____

2. Naomi is ordering T-shirts for the school fundraiser. The graph represents the cost of the T-shirts.

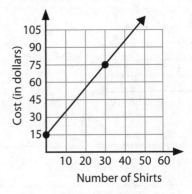

    a. What is the initial fee? _____

    b. What is the cost per shirt? _____

    c. Write an equation to represent the cost of the T-shirts.

        $y =$ _____

3. Raisa is looking at prices for a cleaning service. The graph shows the cost of the service.

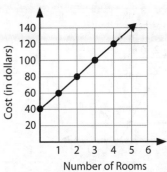

    a. What is the initial fee that the service charges? _____

    b. What is the cost of cleaning per room? _____

    c. Write an equation to represent the cost of the cleaning service.

        $y =$ _____

4. Rohan buys pet supplies every month for his pet rabbit. The amount of money he spends is shown on the graph.

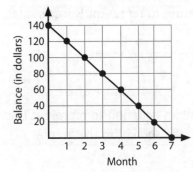

    a. How much money did Rohan start with in his account? _____

    b. How much does Rohan spend each month? _____

    c. Write an equation to represent the amount in Rohan's bank account.

        $y =$ _____

Rate of Change

Name: _____   Date: _____

Directions: Solve each problem.

1. Write an equation to represent the function shown on the graph.

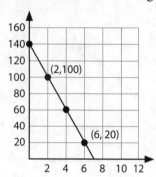

y = _____

2. Write an equation to represent the function shown in the table.

x	0	30	60	90
y	35	305	575	900

y = _____

3. Rocco sells his artwork in an online store. He charges $11 per item plus a shipping fee of $3.50. Write an equation to represent Rocco's sales.

y = _____

4. Write an equation to represent the function shown on the graph.

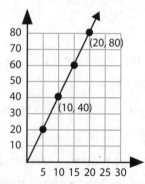

y = _____

5. Write an equation to represent the function shown in the table.

x	−5	0	5	10
y	−28	12	52	92

y = _____

6. Reva noticed that her tomato plant was growing at a constant rate for a few days. The plant was 3 inches tall when she bought it. The plant grew 2 inches per day while Reva recorded the height. Write an equation to represent the growth of the tomato plant.

y = _____

7. What is the equation represented by the graph?

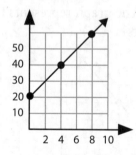

y = _____

8. Write an equation to represent the function shown in the table.

x	−10	0	10	20
y	−240	60	360	660

y = _____

Rate of Change

Learn about Graphing Functional Relationships

A **graph** is a visual representation of data represented in an organized manner that is easy to understand. Graphs of functions can be increasing, decreasing, or remaining the same. Graphs can also be proportional or not proportional.

A proportional graph must be a straight line that passes through the origin, (0, 0).

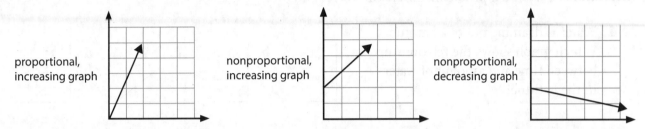

proportional, increasing graph

nonproportional, increasing graph

nonproportional, decreasing graph

Graphs can also be linear or nonlinear. A linear graph is a straight line. A nonlinear graph is not a straight line.

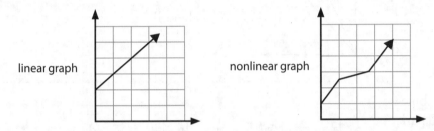

linear graph

nonlinear graph

Example 1

Micah is filling his fish tank with water at a constant rate. Draw a graph that represents the amount of water in the tank over time.

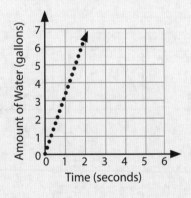

1. Identify the variables. In this case, the variables are *time* and the *amount of water* in the fish tank. Time should be labeled on the *x*-axis, and the amount of water should be labeled on the *y*-axis.

2. Determine whether the graph is proportional. Will it be a straight line and go through point (0, 0)? _____

3. Determine whether the graph should be increasing or decreasing. As time passes, does the amount of water increase or decrease? _____

4. Trace the line on the graph to show the relationship between time and water in the tank.

Name: _____ **Date:** _____

✐ Quick Tip

Deciding whether the graph should be increasing, decreasing, or remaining consistent can help you choose the correct graph.

Directions: Solve each problem. Circle the correct answer.

1. Water is draining out of a bathtub. Which graph shows the relationship between time and amount of water in the bathtub?

   a.   **b.**   **c.**   **d.**

2. Two friends are riding their bikes to the park. Their routes are shown on the graph.

   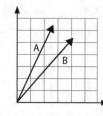

   Which friend was riding faster?
   a. Friend A
   b. Friend B

3. Roger was quickly riding his bike to the park. He stayed at the park for a while and then rode quickly to his friend's house. Which graph represents the relationship between time and the distance Roger traveled?

   a.   **b.**   **c.**   **d.**

4. The amount of money in Ria's bank account is decreasing at the same rate each month. Which graph represents the relationship between time and the the amount of money in Ria's account?

   a.   **b.**   **c.**   **d.**

5. Tia left school and walked to her friend's house, where she stayed for a while. Her friend's house is on the way to her house. Which graph represents the relationship between time and distance away from Tia's house?

   a.   **b.**   **c.**   **d.**

6. Mia stayed at her grandmother's house all day. Which graph represents the relationship between time and distance from Mia's home?

   a.   **b.**   **c.**   **d.**

Name: _____ Date: _____

Directions: Complete the tasks, and answer the questions.

1. Raoul's pool is filling up at a constant rate. Draw a graph to represent the relationship between time and water in the pool.

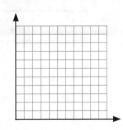

Is the graph linear or nonlinear?

_____

2. Kennedy ran from her house to the park, stayed for a while, and then walked home. Draw a graph to represent Kennedy's time and distance from her house.

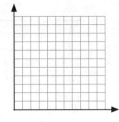

Is the graph linear or nonlinear?

_____

3. Li's water bottle had a slow leak in it. Draw a graph to represent the relationship between time and water remaining in the bottle.

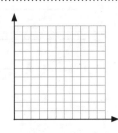

Is the graph linear or nonlinear?

_____

4. Mya walked to the tennis courts from her house. She played tennis for a while and then jogged to her friend's house, which is past the tennis courts. Draw a graph to represent the relationship between time and the distance Mya is from home.

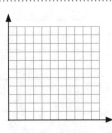

Is the graph linear or nonlinear?

_____

5. Shen is saving money for college. He saves the same amount each month. Draw a graph to represent the relationship between time and the amount of money Shen has saved.

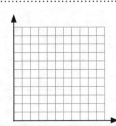

Is the graph linear or nonlinear?

_____

6. Tya filled up the bathtub, took a bath, and then drained the water out of the tub. The tub fills up and drains at the same rate. Draw a graph to represent the relationship between time and the amount of water in the bathtub.

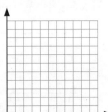

Is the graph linear or nonlinear?

_____

Graphing Functional Relationships

Name: _____ **Date:** _____

Directions: Write a scenario to match each graph.

1.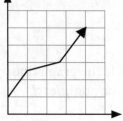

_____

_____

_____

2.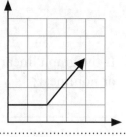

_____

_____

_____

3.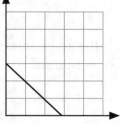

_____

_____

_____

4.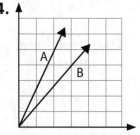

_____

_____

_____

5.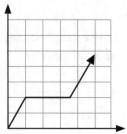

_____

_____

_____

6.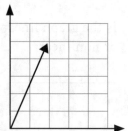

_____

_____

_____

Directions: Circle whether each relationship is linear or nonlinear.

1. Tremaine is walking at a constant rate to school.

   linear   nonlinear

2. The coffee pot filled up as the coffee brewed. Marcus and his family drank all of the coffee when it was finished brewing.

   linear   nonlinear

3. Suri was riding her bike to the park. She got a flat tire, so she waited for her parents to pick her up. Then, she rode home in her parents' car.

   linear   nonlinear

4. Henrietta is baking cookies. Each hour, she makes another batch of cookies.

   linear   nonlinear

5. Garrett saved $90 each month and put it into his savings account.

   linear   nonlinear

6. Vern spent money on entertainment each month. Some months he spent more money than others.

   linear   nonlinear

7. A tree was growing at a constant rate all summer.

   linear   nonlinear

8. Every time one of the students in Mrs. Jones's class scored a perfect score on a test, she put a marble in a bottle. Once the bottle was full, the class had a party.

   linear   nonlinear

9. Quin walked for 4 days. On day 1, he walked 1 mile. On day 2, he walked 4 miles. On day 3, he walked 9 miles, and on day 4, he walked 16 miles.

   linear   nonlinear

10. Every week, Mariah knitted 2 more scarves than she did the week before.

    linear   nonlinear

Graphing Functional Relationships

Name: _____ **Date:** _____

Directions: Solve each problem.

1. Lou spends $14 each month on snacks for his dog. Which graph represents the amount of money left in Lou's bank account each month, if that is all he spends money on? Circle the answer.

a. c.

b. d.

4. Write a story to match the graph.

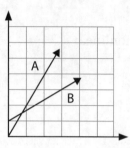

_____

_____

_____

_____

2. Bryan walked from home to the ice cream shop, stayed there, ate an ice cream cone, and then walked home. Sketch a graph of Bryan's distance from home over time.

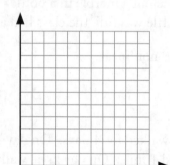

5. Amalya is filling a pitcher of lemonade at a constant rate. Which graph shows the relationship of the amount of lemonade in the pitcher over time?

a. c.

b. d.

3. Kylie roller-skated to the skate park at a steady rate. What type of relationship is this?

linear   nonlinear

6. Carmen left school, went to the post office to drop off a card to mail, and then went home. Sketch a graph to represent Carmen's distance from home during her afternoon. Then, circle whether it is linear or nonlinear.

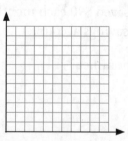

linear   nonlinear

Name: _____ Date: _____

Directions: Solve each problem.

1. $\dfrac{m^3}{m^2} =$ _____

2. $2(9 - 10)^2 + \dfrac{1}{2}(4 - 6) - 10 =$ _____

3. Solve and graph the solution on the number line.

   $4x - 10 < 30$

   a. Solution: x _____

   b.
   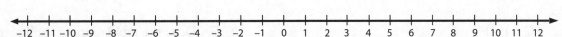

4. Write $\dfrac{5}{8}$ as a decimal.

   _____

5. Plot the approximate locations of the numbers, and graph them on the number line.
   $\sqrt{67}, \sqrt{89}, \sqrt{78}$

   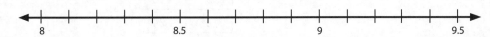

6. $x^3 = 729$

   $x =$ _____

7. Does the graph show a proportional relationship?

   _____

   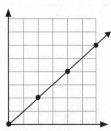

8. Is the relationship a function?

   _____

Input	Output
−2	0
5	1
8	2

9. Write 87,000,000 in scientific notation.

   _____

10. What is $4.\overline{6}$ written as a fraction?

    _____

Name: _____   Date: _____

Directions: Solve each problem.

1. Does the graph show a function?

_____

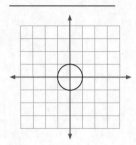

2. $(x^4)^5 =$ _____

3. Write the numbers from least to greatest.

$-3\frac{1}{8}, -\sqrt{6}, \frac{-23}{8}, -3.9$

_____

4. $(2.6 \times 10^4)(1.7 \times 10^3) =$ _____

5. Find the range for the domain of the function.

$y = 4x + 3$

Domain: 0, 1, 2, 3, 4

Range: _____

6. $x^2 = 100$

$x =$ _____

7. Does the table represent a linear function?

_____

x	y
1	–6
2	–12
3	–18
4	–24

8. $\frac{2}{5}(10x - 15) + 4 = 3(x + 2)$

$x =$ _____

9. Does the graph show a proportional relationship?

_____

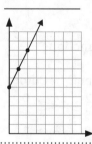

10. $6^3 - 6^2 =$ _____

Directions: Solve each problem.

1. $(6.5 \times 10^6) - (4.3 \times 10^6) =$ _____

2. Is the relationship shown in the table a function?

   _____

x	y
1	4
2	4
3	3
4	2

3. $9^3 =$ _____

4. Janice jogs 3 miles every day.

   a. Make a graph of the proportional relationship between the number of days Janice runs and the total number of miles she has run.

   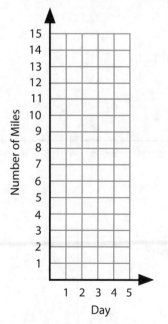

   Day

   b. What is the slope of the line?

   _____

5. $(8.7 \times 10^9) + (1.4 \times 10^8) =$ _____

6. Is (6, 6) a solution to the system of equations?

   $y + \frac{1}{3}x = 8$

   $y = \frac{1}{6}x + 5$

   _____

7. $\sqrt{x^4 y^8} =$ _____

8. $4(x + 6) = 2x - 15 + 3(x - 4)$

   $x =$ _____

9. $\dfrac{y^9 z^{12}}{y^8 z^{11}} =$ _____

10. Write 8.5×10^{-6} in standard form.

    _____

Name: _____ Date: _____

Directions: Solve each problem.

1. $\dfrac{(9.6 \times 10^5)}{(3.2 \times 10^4)} =$ _____

2. $\triangle ABC \sim \triangle FGE$

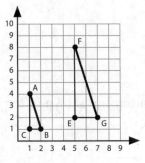

   a. What is the slope of line AB? _____

   b. What is the slope of line FG? _____

3. Is the relationship on the graph proportional?

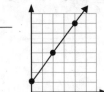

4. Write an equation for the line.

   $y =$ _____

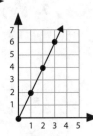

5. Solve the system of equations algebraically.

   $y = 2x + 3$

   $-2x + y = 9$

   Solution: _____

6. Solve the inequality, and graph the solution on the number line.

   $5(x + 4) - 10 \leq 3(x - 2)$

   a. Solution: x _____

   b.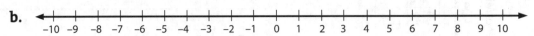

7. Write $0.\overline{8}$ as a fraction.

   _____

8. Is the relationship shown on the graph linear or nonlinear?

   _____

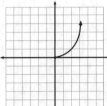

9. Write 5.7×10^6 in standard form. _____

10. $\sqrt[3]{512} =$ _____

Directions: Solve each problem.

1. Is the point (2, 1) a solution to the system of equations?

$6x + y = 13$

$y = 4x - 7$

_____

2. $(8.3 \times 10^4) - (5.2 \times 10^3) =$ _____

3. $9(12 - 14) + 4^2 - 6(9 - 12) + 3^2 =$ _____

4. Mikhail is downloading music from an online provider. The graph represents the cost of downloads.

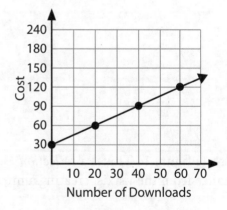

Number of Downloads

a. What is the initial fee? _____

b. What is the cost per download?

_____

c. Write an equation to represent the cost of any number of downloads. Use c for cost and n for number of downloads. _____

5. Write a story that describes the graph.

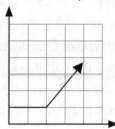

_____

_____

6. $x^2 = 144$

$x =$ _____

7. Which two integers is $\sqrt{5}$ between?

_____

8. Write an equation for the line.

$y =$ _____

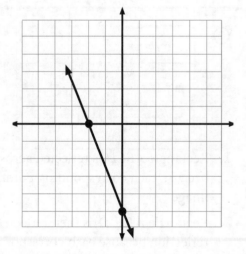

Spiral Review

Learn about Transformations

A **transformation** is the change in size or location of a shape on a plane.

- A **rotation** is a type of transformation where a figure rotates a certain number of degrees around a fixed point. The size and shape of the figure remain the same.

- A **reflection** is a type of transformation where an object is flipped over a fixed line, creating a mirror image that is congruent to the original figure.

- A **translation**, also known as a slide, is a type of transformation that moves a figure up, down, left, or right but does not turn the shape. The size and orientation remain the same.

- A **dilation** is a type of transformation that changes the size of a figure by increasing or decreasing the dimensions by a scale factor.

A **scale factor** is a number that all of the dimensions of a figure are multiplied by to find the dimensions of a new figure.

Two shapes are **congruent** if they are identical in shape and size.

Two shapes are **similar** if they are the same shape, have congruent corresponding angle measures, and the ratios of the lengths of their corresponding sides are congruent.

Example 1

Identify the transformation.

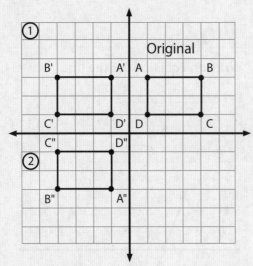

1. Rectangle *ABCD* is reflected across the *y*-axis to create figure 1. This is a *reflection* because each corresponding point is the same distance from the *y*-axis, creating a mirror image.

2. Rectangle *A'B'C'D'* is then reflected across the *x*-axis to create figure 2. This is another reflection because each corresponding point is the same distance from the *x*-axis, creating a mirror image.

Learn about Transformations *(cont.)*

Example 2

Rectangle *ABCD* is rotated 90° around the origin. Compare *ABCD* to rectangle *A'B'C'D'*.

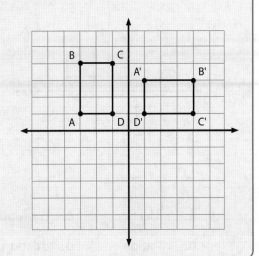

1. The length of *AB* and *A'B'* are both
    _____ units.

2. The width of *BC* and *B'C'* are both
    _____ units.

3. Side *AB* is congruent to side *DC*, so side *A'B'* is
    congruent to side *D'C'*.

4. Are rectangle *ABCD* and rectangle *A'B'C'D'*
    congruent? _____

Example 3

Draw a dilation of the figure with a scale factor of 2.

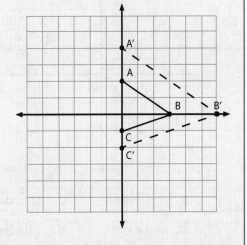

1. First, identify the coordinates of each point.

    A (0, 2)

    B (3, 0)

    C (0, –1)

2. Multiply each number by 2 to find the new
    coordinates.

    A' (0, 4)

    B' (6, 0)

    C' (0, –2)

3. Trace the lines of triangle *A'B'C'* on the graph.

Name: _____ Date: _____

Directions: Identify each type of transformation. Circle your answer.

1.

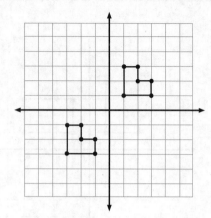

a. reflection   c. translation

b. rotation   d. dilation

4.

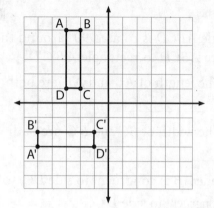

a. reflection   c. translation

b. rotation   d. dilation

2.

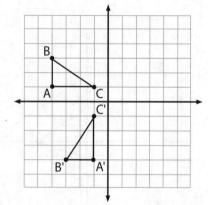

a. reflection   c. translation

b. rotation   d. dilation

5.

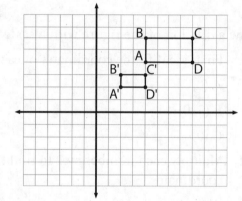

a. reflection   c. translation

b. rotation   d. dilation

3.

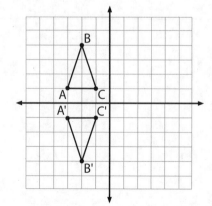

a. reflection   c. translation

b. rotation   d. dilation

6.

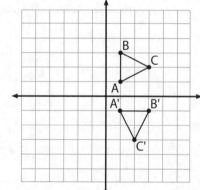

a. reflection   c. translation

b. rotation   d. dilation

Transformations

Directions: Determine the number of degrees each diagram was rotated around the origin, and then answer the questions.

1. How many degrees was rectangle *XYZW* rotated clockwise around the origin to create rectangle *X'Y'Z'W'*?

_____

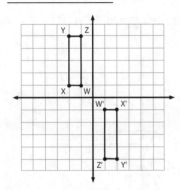

a. On rectangle *XYZW*, which side is parallel to *XY*? _____

b. On rectangle *X'Y'Z'W'*, which side is parallel to *X'Y'*? _____

c. If side *XW* is 1 unit, what is the length of side *X'W'*? _____

d. Are the angles from rectangle *X'Y'Z'W'* congruent to the corresponding angles from rectangle *XYZW*? _____

2. How many degrees was triangle *ABC* rotated counterclockwise around the origin to create triangle *A'B'C'*?

_____

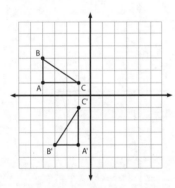

a. On triangle *ABC*, which side is perpendicular to side *AC*? _____

b. On triangle *A'B'C'*, which side is perpendicular to side *A'C'*? _____

c. If side *AC* is 3 units, what is the length of side *A'C'*? _____

d. Are the angles from triangle *A'B'C'* congruent to the corresponding angles from triangle *ABC*?

_____

3. How many degrees was triangle *ABC* rotated clockwise around the origin to create triangle *A'B'C'*?

_____

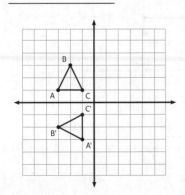

a. Which side corresponds to side *AB* from triangle *A'B'C'*? _____

b. Which side corresponds to side *BC* from triangle *A'B'C'*? _____

c. If side *AC* is 2 units, what is the length of side *A'C'*? _____

d. Are the angles from triangle *A'B'C'* congruent to the corresponding angles from triangle *ABC*?

_____

Transformations

Name: _____   Date: _____

Directions: Complete each task.

1. Dilate rectangle *WXYZ* by a scale factor of $\frac{1}{2}$.

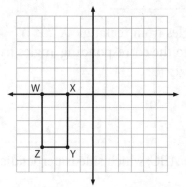

2. Dilate parallelogram *ABCD* by a scale factor of 3.

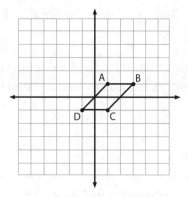

3. Dilate rectangle *ABCD* by a scale factor of $\frac{1}{3}$.

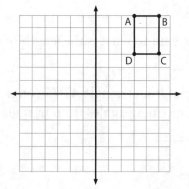

4. Dilate parallelogram *MNOP* by a scale factor of 3.

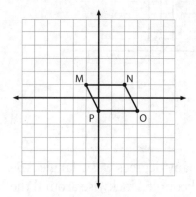

5. Dilate triangle *XYZ* by a scale factor of 2.

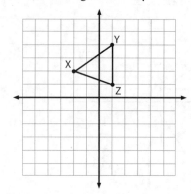

6. Dilate square *GHJK* by a scale factor of $\frac{1}{4}$.

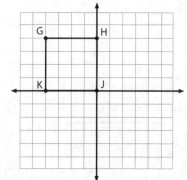

Transformations

🖎 Quick Tip

Remember, a rotation is a turn of 90°, 180°, 270°, or 360°. A translation is a slide in the direction and number of units given. A reflection is a flip across the *x*- or *y*-axis.

Directions: Draw each transformation on the coordinate grid.

1. Translate the figure to the right 5.

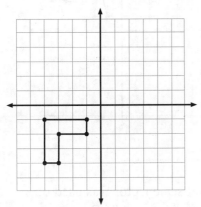

4. Rotate the figure clockwise 180°.

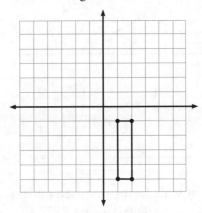

2. Rotate the figure 90° clockwise around the origin.

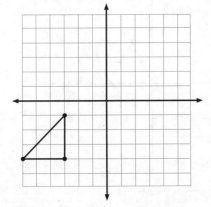

5. Translate the figure down 5.

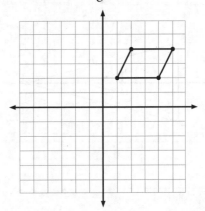

3. Reflect the figure over the *y*-axis.

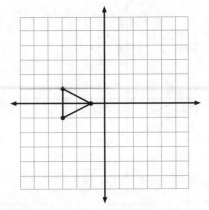

6. Reflect the figure across the *x*-axis.

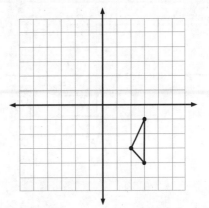

Transformations

Name: _____ Date: _____

Directions: Answer the questions.

1. What scale factor was used on triangle *ABC* to create triangle *A'B'C'*?

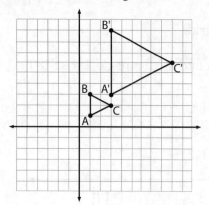

_____

2. What scale factor was used on triangle *ABC* to create triangle *A'B'C'*?

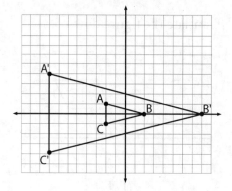

_____

3. What scale factor was used on rectangle *ABCD* to create rectangle *A'B'C'D'*?

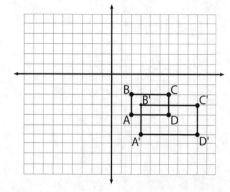

_____

4. What scale factor was used on triangle *ABC* to create triangle *A'B'C'*?

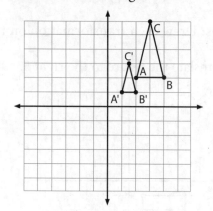

_____

5. What scale factor was used on parallelogram *ABCD* to create parallelogram *A'B'C'D'*?

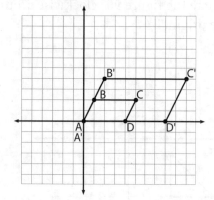

_____

6. What scale factor was used on triangle *XYZ* to create triangle *X'Y'Z'*?

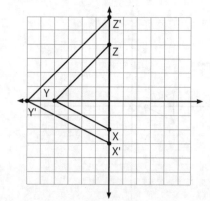

_____

Directions: Determine the two transformations that occurred to move figure 1 to figure 2.

1. _____ and _____

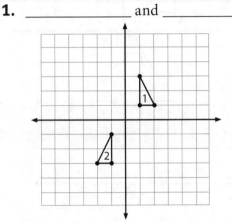

4. _____ and _____

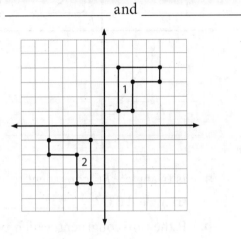

2. _____ and _____

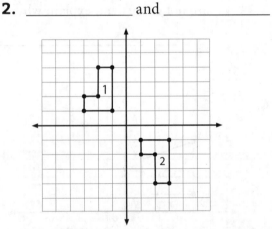

5. _____ and _____

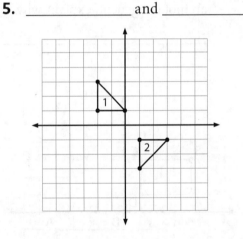

3. _____ and _____

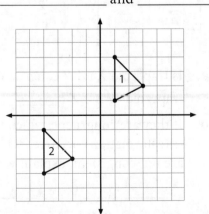

6. _____ and _____

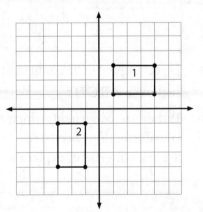

Transformations

Transformations

Directions: Solve each problem.

1.

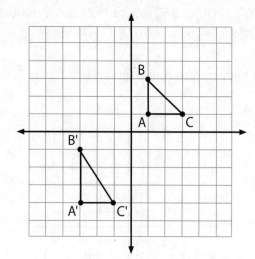

a. Is triangle *ABC* congruent to triangle *A'B'C'*? _____

b. If they are congruent, which two transformations occurred? If they are not congruent, explain why.

_____

3.

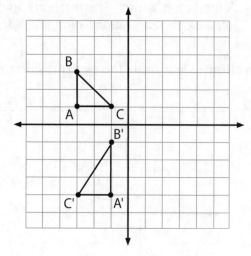

a. Is triangle *ABC* congruent to triangle *A'B'C'*? _____

b. If they are congruent, which two transformations occurred? If they are not congruent, explain why.

_____

2.

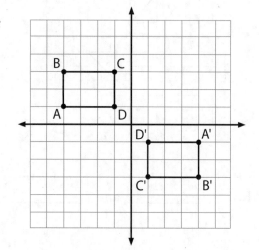

a. Is rectangle *ABCD* congruent to rectangle *A'B'C'D'*? _____

b. If they are congruent, which two transformations occurred? If they are not congruent, explain why.

_____

4.

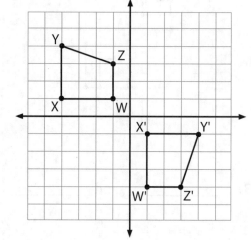

a. Is trapezoid *XYZW* congruent to trapezoid *W'X'Y'Z'*? _____

b. If they are congruent, which two transformations occurred? If they are not congruent, explain why.

_____

> 🖉 **Quick Tip**
>
> The symbol for *congruent* is ≅. The symbol for *similar* or to show similarity
> is ~. If two triangles are congruent, you can write △ *ABC* ≅ △ *A'B'C'*. If
> two triangles are similar, you can write △ *ABC* ~ △ *A'B'C'*.

Directions: Answer the questions.

1.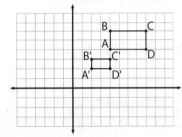

   a. Are the rectangles congruent? _____

   b. Are the rectangles similar? _____

   c. What is the area of rectangle *ABCD*? _____

   d. What is the area of rectangle *A'B'C'D'*?

      _____

2.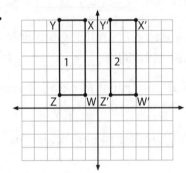

   a. Are the rectangles congruent? _____

   b. What transformation was done to rectangle 1 to create
      rectangle 2? _____

   c. angle *W* ≅ _____

   d. side *ZY* ≅ _____

3.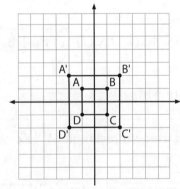

   a. Are the squares congruent? _____

   b. Are the squares similar? _____

   c. What is the length of side *AB*? _____

   d. What is the length of side *A'B'*? _____

4.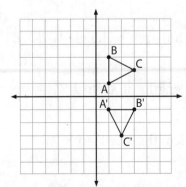

   a. Are the triangles congruent? _____

   b. What transformation was done to triangle *ABC* to
      create triangle *A'B'C'*? _____

   c. angle *B* ≅ _____

   d. side *BC* ≅ _____

Transformations

Name: _____ Date: _____

Directions: Solve each problem.

1.

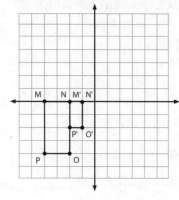

a. What scale factor was used on rectangle *MNOP* to create rectangle *M'N'O'P'*? _____

b. Is rectangle *MNOP* congruent to rectangle *M'N'O'P'*? _____

c. Is rectangle *MNOP* similar to rectangle *M'N'O'P'*? _____

d. Write a ratio for the lengths of *MN* to *MP*. _____

e. Write a ratio for the lengths of *M'N'* to *M'P'*. _____

f. Are the ratios proportional? _____

2.

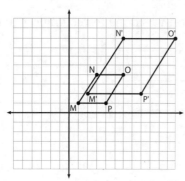

a. What scale factor was used on parallelogram *MNOP* to create parallelogram *M'N'O'P'*? _____

b. Is parallelogram *MNOP* congruent to parallelogram *M'N'O'P'*? _____

c. Is parallelogram *MNOP* similar to parallelogram *M'N'O'P'*? _____

d. Write a ratio for the height of *MNOP* to the length of *MP*. _____

e. Write a ratio for the height of *M'N'O'P'* to the length of *M'P'*. _____

f. Are the ratios proportional? _____

3.

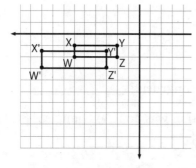

a. What scale factor was used on rectangle *WXYZ* to create rectangle *W'X'Y'Z'*? _____

b. Is rectangle *WXYZ* congruent to rectangle *W'X'Y'Z'*? _____

c. Is rectangle *WXYZ* similar to rectangle *W'X'Y'Z'*? _____

d. Write a ratio for the lengths of *XY* to *XW*. _____

e. Write a ratio for the lengths of *X'Y'* to *X'W'*. _____

f. Are the ratios proportional? _____

Directions: Solve each problem.

1.

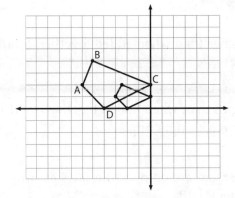

a. What transformation created the smaller shape from the larger shape?

_____

b. Are the shapes congruent? _____

c. Are the shapes similar? If so, what scale factor was used on quadrilateral *ABCD* to get the smaller quadrilateral?

_____

3.

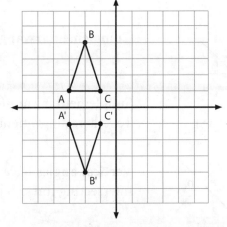

a. What transformation created triangle *A'B'C'* from triangle *ABC*?

_____

b. Complete the congruency statement.
AC ≅ _____

2.

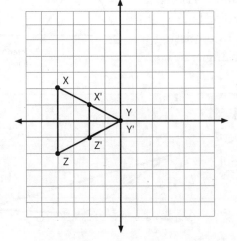

a. What transformation created triangle *X'Y'Z'* from triangle *XYZ*?

_____

b. Are the shapes congruent? _____

c. Are the shapes similar? If so, what scale factor was used on triangle *XYZ* to get triangle *X'Y'Z'*?

_____

4.

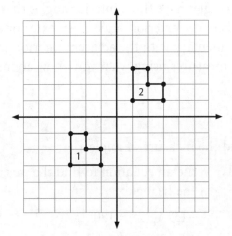

a. What transformation(s) occurred to figure 1 to create figure 2?

_____

b. Are the shapes congruent?

_____

Transformations

Learn about Angle Relationships
Types of Angles

Complementary angles are two angles that, when added together, total 90°.

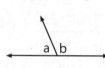

Supplementary angles are two angles that, when added together, total 180°. Together, supplementary angles form a straight angle.

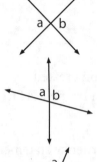

Vertical angles have the same vertex but are on opposite sides of two intersecting lines. They are congruent.

Adjacent angles have a common side and a common vertex. Their measures add to 180°.

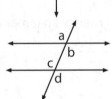

Corresponding angles are formed at corresponding corners when two parallel lines are intersected by a transversal. They are congruent. In this diagram, angles *a* and *c* are corresponding, and angles *b* and *d* are corresponding.

Triangles

All triangles have three interior angles that total exactly 180°. Triangles can also have exterior angles. An exterior angle on a triangle is supplementary with the adjacent interior angle. You can find missing angle measures using what you know about angles and triangles.

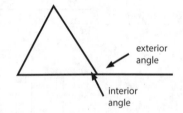

Example 1

Find the measure of angle *x*.

1. Write an equation to find the missing interior angle of the triangle.

   $y + 15° + 12° = 180°$

2. Solve the equation.

   $y = 153°$

3. Write another equation to find the exterior angle. Use your answer from step 2.

   $x + 153° = 180°$

4. Solve the equation.

   $x = $ _____

Learn about Angle Relationships *(cont.)*

Example 2

Find the missing angle measures.

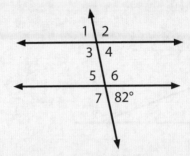

1. First, find the measure of angle 7. Angle 7 and angle 8 are supplementary, so you can write and solve this equation:

   $x + 82° = 180°$

   $x = 98°$

2. Write the missing measures using what you know about angle relationships.

   • Angle 6 and angle 7 are vertical angles, so angle 6 = 98°.

   • Angle 5 and the given angle are vertical angles, so angle 5 = 82°.

   • Angle 1 is a corresponding angle to angle 5, so angle 1 is also 82°.

   • The measures of angles 2, 3, and 4 can also be found by looking at their corresponding angles. So, angle 2 = 98°, angle 3 = 98°, and angle 4 = 82°.

Name: _____   Date: _____

🖐 Quick Tip

Remember, the three interior angles in every triangle must add up to exactly 180°. Supplementary angles also add up to exactly 180°.

Directions: Find the missing exterior angles.

1. x = _____

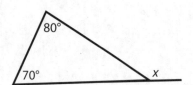

2. x = _____

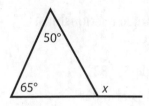

3. x = _____

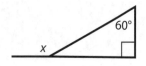

4. x = _____

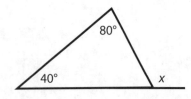

5. x = _____

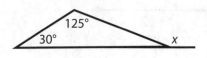

6. x = _____

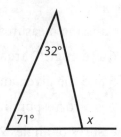

7. x = _____

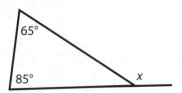

8. x = _____

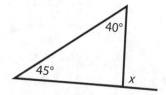

Directions: Find the missing angle measures.

1. Angle 1 = _____

2. Angle 2 = _____

3. Angle 3 = _____

4. Angle 4 = _____

5. Angle 5 = _____

6. Angle 6 = _____

7. Angle 7 = _____

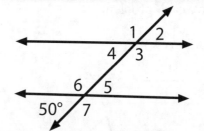

Directions: Find the missing angle measures.

8. Angle 1 = _____

9. Angle 2 = _____

10. Angle 3 = _____

11. Angle 4 = _____

12. Angle 5 = _____

13. Angle 6 = _____

14. Angle 7 = _____

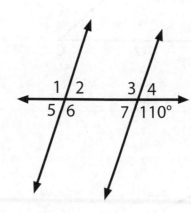

Angle Relationships

Name: _____   Date: _____

Directions: Solve each problem.

1. Is Δ *ABC* ~ Δ *XYZ*?

_____

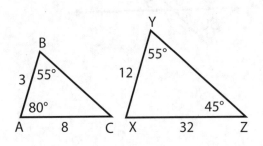

4. Is Δ *ABC* ~ Δ *DEF*?

_____

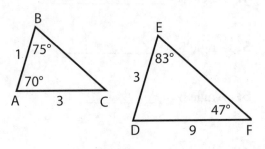

2. Is Δ *ABC* ~ Δ *XBY*?

_____

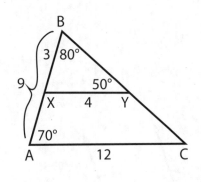

5. Is Δ *MNO* ~ Δ *JKL*?

_____

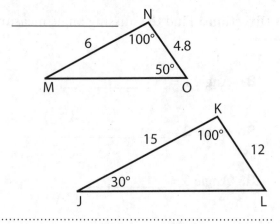

3. Is Δ *WTZ* ~ Δ *YXZ*?

_____

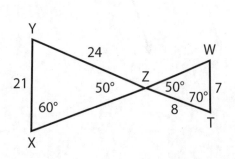

6. Is Δ *ABC* ~ Δ *DBE*?

_____

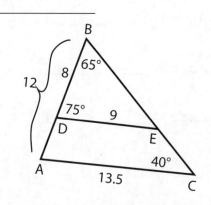

Name: _____ **Date:** _____

✏️ Quick Tip

Any polygon can be divided into triangles by drawing a diagonal from one vertex to every other vertex. The angle sum in any polygon can be found using the formula $180(n-2)$, where n is the number of sides on the polygon.

A square has 4 sides, so you substitute 4 for n into the expression $180(n-2)$.

$180(4-2) = 180(2) = 360$

There are 360° in any quadrilateral (four-sided polygon).

Directions: Solve each problem. Use the diagrams to help you find the angle sums.

1. angle sum: _____

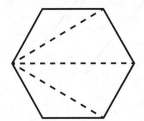

2. angle sum: _____

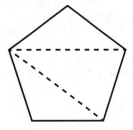

· ·

Directions: Draw the diagonals in these polygons, and find the angle sums.

3. angle sum: _____

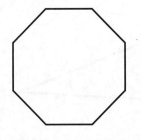

5. angle sum: _____

4. angle sum: _____

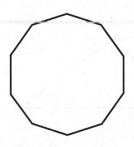

6. angle sum: _____

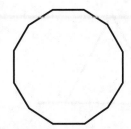

Angle Relationships

Name: _____   Date: _____

> 📝 **Reminder**
>
> A **transversal** is a line that intersects two or more parallel lines.

Directions: Solve each problem. Use the following diagram to answer problems 1–6.

1. Identify two pairs of supplementary angles.

   _____ and _____

2. Identify two pairs of vertical angles.

   _____ and _____

3. Identify two pairs of corresponding angles.

   _____ and _____

4. Identify the transversal.

   _____

5. What is the measure of angle 2?

   _____

6. What is the measure of angle 5?

   _____

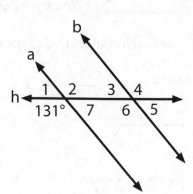

Angle Relationships

- -

7. What is the measure of angle *x*?

   x = _____

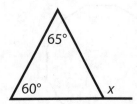

9. What is the measure of angle *x*?

   x = _____

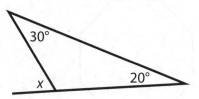

8. What is the measure of angle *x*?

   x = _____

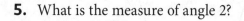

10. What is the measure of angle *x*?

   x = _____

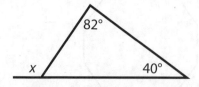

Learn about the Pythagorean Theorem

The two sides of a right triangle that form the right angle are called the **legs**, while the diagonal side opposite of the right angle is called the **hypotenuse**. The hypotenuse is the longest side of a right triangle. The legs are sides a and b, while the hypotenuse is side c.

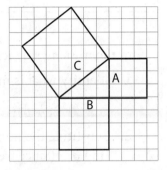

The **Pythagorean Theorem** states that the square of the length of the hypotenuse is equal to the sum of the squares of the legs.

$$a^2 + b^2 = c^2$$

Example 1

Use the Pythagorean Theorem to find the missing side.

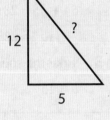

1. Identify the legs on the triangle. (12 and 5)

2. Substitute the values into the equation.

$$a^2 + b^2 = c^2$$
$$12^2 + 5^2 = c^2$$
$$144 + 25 = c^2$$

3. Add the squares together.

$$169 = c^2$$

4. Find the square root to solve for c. This is the length of the hypotenuse.

$$c = 13$$

Example 2

The Pythagorean Theorem can also be used to prove that a triangle is a right triangle.

For example, a triangle has lengths 3, 4, and 5. Is it a right triangle?

1. Substitute the numbers into the equation.

$$3^2 + 4^2 = 5^2$$
$$9 + 16 = 25$$
$$25 = 25$$

2. Is the equation true?

Yes, the triangle is a right triangle.

Learn about the Pythagorean Theorem (cont.)

Example 3

Find the missing side length on the right triangle.

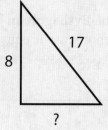

1. Identify what is missing. Is a leg or the hypotenuse missing?

   _____

2. Substitute the numbers into the equation. Solve the equation to find b^2. (Since we are solving for a leg, either a or b could be used.)

   $a^2 + b^2 = c^2$

   $8^2 + b^2 = 17$

   $64 + b^2 = 289$

   $b^2 = 225$

3. Take the square root of both sides of the equation.

   $b = 15$

Example 4

Find the distance between the two points in the coordinate plane.

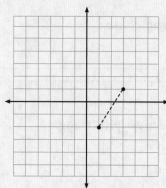

1. Connect the two points with a line segment.

2. Draw a right triangle. The line segment connecting the two points is the hypotenuse. Count and label the length of leg a and leg b.

3. Use the Pythagorean Theorem to find the length of the hypotenuse.

   $a^2 + b^2 = c^2$

   $2^2 + 3^2 = c^2$

   $4 + 9 = c^2$

   $13 = c^2$

   $\sqrt{13} = c$

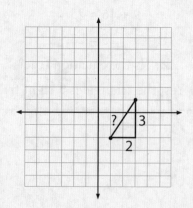

Name: _____ **Date:** _____

Directions: Find the hypotenuse of each triangle using the Pythagorean Theorem. Write the answer as a square root, or approximate the square root to the hundredths place.

1. $c =$ _____

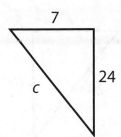

2. $c =$ _____

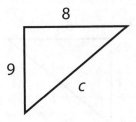

3. $c =$ _____

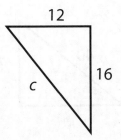

4. $c =$ _____

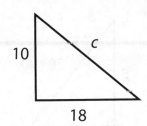

5. $c =$ _____

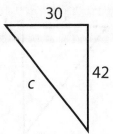

6. $c =$ _____

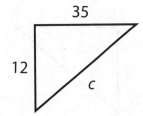

7. $c =$ _____

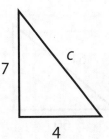

8. $c =$ _____

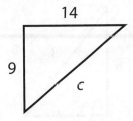

Pythagorean Theorem

142250—180 Days of Math

Name: _____ Date: _____

Directions: Find the missing leg on each right triangle. Write the answer as a square root, or approximate the square root to the hundredths place.

1. $a =$ _____

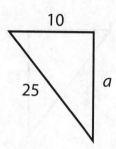

5. $a =$ _____

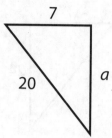

2. $a =$ _____

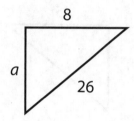

6. $a =$ _____

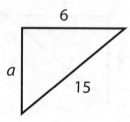

3. $a =$ _____

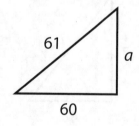

7. $a =$ _____

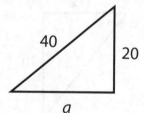

4. $a =$ _____

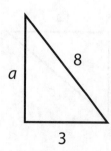

8. $a =$ _____

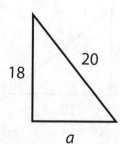

142250—180 Days of Math   © Shell Education

Directions: Circle whether each triangle formed with the given side lengths is a right triangle.

1. yes   no

$a = 27$
$b = 36$
$c - 45$

2. yes   no

$a = 15$
$b = 8$
$c = 19$

3. yes   no

$a = 12$
$b = 16$
$c = 20$

4. yes   no

$a = 5$
$b = 11$
$c = 29$

5. yes   no

$a = 9$
$b = 12$
$c = 16$

6. yes   no

$a = 10$
$b = 24$
$c = 26$

7. yes   no

$a = 32$
$b = 24$
$c = 40$

8. yes   no

$a = 6$
$b = 8$
$c = 10$

Pythagorean Theorem

Name: _____ Date: _____

Directions: Find the distance *c* between the two points using the Pythagorean Theorem. (Connect the dots to form a hypotenuse. Find the lengths of sides *a* and *b*. Then, solve for *c*.)

1. $c =$ _____

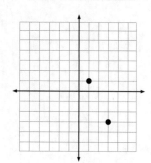

2. $c =$ _____

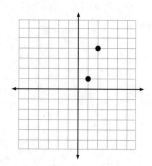

3. $c =$ _____

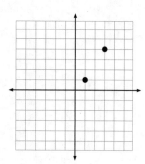

4. $c =$ _____

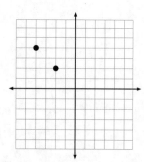

5. $c =$ _____

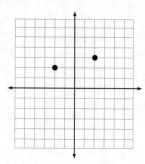

6. $c =$ _____

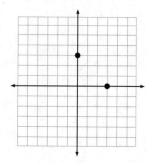

7. $c =$ _____

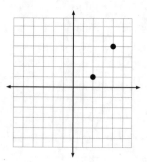

8. $c =$ _____

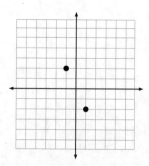

142250—180 Days of Math

Name: _____ **Date:** _____

Directions: Find the missing side length in each of the right triangles. Write the answer as a square root, or approximate the square root to the hundredths place.

1. $c =$ _____

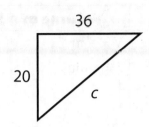

4. $c =$ _____

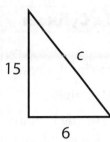

2. $a =$ _____

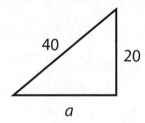

5. $c =$ _____

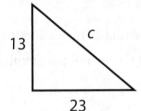

3. $a =$ _____

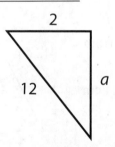

6. $a =$ _____

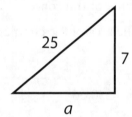

Directions: Find the distance between the two points using the Pythagorean Theorem.

7. $c =$ _____

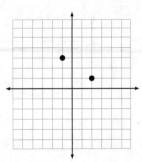

8. $c =$ _____

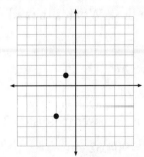

Pythagorean Theorem

Learn about Volume

Volume is the space inside a three-dimensional figure. Volume is labeled in cubic units.

There are different formulas used to calculate the volume of these figures.

Volume of a Cylinder	Volume of a Cone	Volume of a Sphere
$V = \pi r^2 h$ r = radius of the circular base h = height of the cylinder You can also write the formula as $V = Bh$, where B is the area of the base and h is the height.	The volume of a cone is $\frac{1}{3}$ the volume of a cylinder with the same base. $V = \frac{1}{3}\pi r^2 h$ r = radius h = height	$V = \frac{4}{3}\pi r^3$ r = radius

Example 1

Find the volume of the cylinder.

1. Find the area of the circular base.

   $A = \pi r^2$
   $\pi \cdot 3^2 = 28.26$

2. Multiply your answer from step 1 by the height.

   $28.26 \cdot 8 = 226.08 \text{ cm}^3$

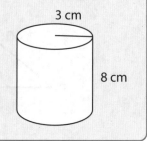

3 cm

8 cm

Example 2

Find the volume of the cone.

1. Find the area of the circular base.

   $A = \pi r^2$
   $\pi \cdot 13^2 = 530.66$

2. Multiply your answer from step 1 by the height.

   $530.66 \cdot 42 = 22{,}287.72$

3. Multiply your answer from step 2 by $\frac{1}{3}$.

   $22{,}287.72 \cdot \frac{1}{3} = 7{,}429.24 \text{ cm}^3$

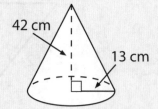

42 cm

13 cm

Example 3

Find the volume of the sphere.

1. Find the radius. What is the radius of the circle?

   6 cm

2. Multiply $\frac{4}{3} \cdot \pi r^3$

   $\pi \cdot 6^3 = 678.24$

3. Multiply your answer from step 2 by $\frac{4}{3}$.

   $\frac{4}{3} \cdot 678.24 = 904.32 \text{ cm}^3$

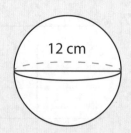

12 cm

Name: _____ **Date:** _____

Directions: Find the volume of each cylinder.

1. V = _____

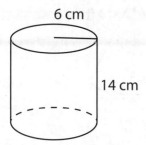

6 cm

14 cm

2. V = _____

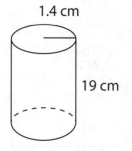

1.4 cm

19 cm

3. V = _____

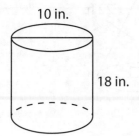

10 in.

18 in.

4. V = _____

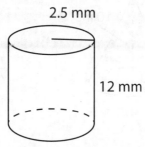

2.5 mm

12 mm

5. V = _____

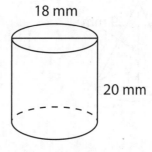

18 mm

20 mm

6. V = _____

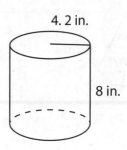

4. 2 in.

8 in.

Volume

Name: _____ Date: _____

Directions: Find the volume of each cone.

1. V = _____

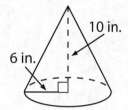

4. V = _____

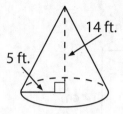

2. V = _____

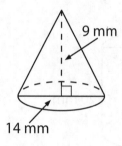

5. V = _____

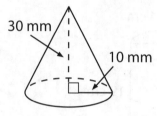

3. V = _____

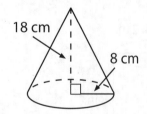

6. V = _____

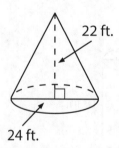

Directions: Find the volume of each sphere.

1. V = _____

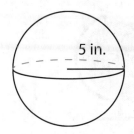

4. V = _____

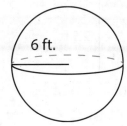

2. V = _____

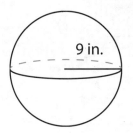

5. V = _____

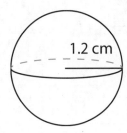

3. V = _____

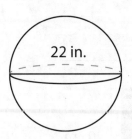

6. V = _____

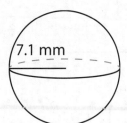

Volume

Name: _____ **Date:** _____

Directions: Find the volume of each figure.

1. V = _____

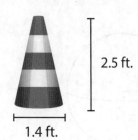

2.5 ft.

1.4 ft.

2. V = _____

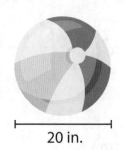

20 in.

3. V = _____

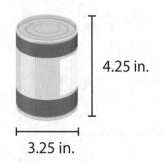

4.25 in.

3.25 in.

4. V = _____

2 in.

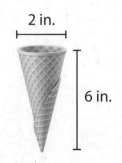

6 in.

5. V = _____

1 ft.

6. V = _____

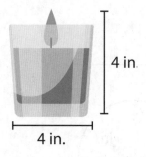

4 in.

4 in.

7. V = _____

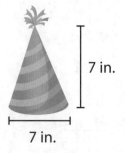

7 in.

7 in.

8. V = _____

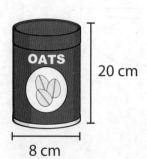

OATS

20 cm

8 cm

Volume

Directions: Read each problem. Draw and label the dimensions of the described shape. Then, find the volume.

1. Miku wants to fill her cylinder fish tank. It has a height of 18 inches and a diameter of 7 inches. How much water will she need to fill the tank?

_____

2. Marcel is preparing cone-shaped containers to fill with bird seed to take to the park. Each cone has a height of 9.5 centimeters and a diameter of 5 centimeters. What is the volume of each cone?

_____

3. Henry is filling his basketball with air. The ball has a radius of 4.7 inches. What is the volume of the basketball?

_____

4. Jacques has a planter shaped like a cylinder that he wants to fill with dirt. The planter has a diameter of 1.5 feet and a height of 3 feet. What is the volume of the planter?

_____

5. Cyrus has a cone-shaped funnel that he wants to fill with motor oil to put in his car engine. The funnel has a radius of 4 inches and a height of 8 inches. What is the volume of the cone?

_____

6. Jade is building a castle out of cardboard for her little brother to play in. The turret is cylinder-shaped with a height of 100 centimeters and a radius of 35 centimeters. What is the volume of the turret?

_____

7. Jade wants to put a cone-shaped roof on the turret (from problem 6). The radius of the cone is 35 centimeters and the height is 60 centimeters. What is the volume of the cone?

_____

8. Deonte is filling a volleyball with air. The volleyball has a diameter of 20.7 centimeters. What is the volume of the volleyball?

_____

Volume

Name: _____   Date: _____

Directions: Solve each problem. Use the following diagram to answer 1–4.

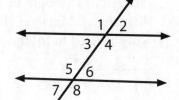

1. Name one pair of vertical angles.

_____

2. Name one pair of supplementary angles.

_____

3. Name one pair of corresponding angles.

_____

4. If angle 3 measures 45°, what is the measure of angle 4?

_____

5. Write $0.\overline{5}$ as a fraction.

_____

6. Plot the decimal approximation for $\sqrt{63}$ on the number line.

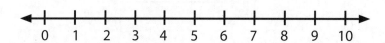

7. What transformations were used to move from figure 1 to figure 2?

_____ and _____

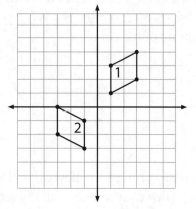

8. $\dfrac{3x^5}{9x^3} =$ _____

9. Order the numbers from least to greatest.

$-3\frac{4}{5}, \frac{-20}{8}, -3.2, 3\frac{1}{5}$

_____

10. Write $\frac{33}{8}$ as a decimal.

_____

Spiral Review

Directions: Solve each problem.

1. Write $33\frac{1}{5}$ as a ratio and a decimal.

    a. Ratio: _____

    b. Decimal: _____

5. $4(x - 6) + 3(2x + 4) = 2(x - 6)$

    $x =$ _____

2. Plot the approximate location of $\sqrt{58}$ on the number line.

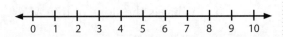

6. Is the relationship represented on the graph linear or nonlinear?

_____

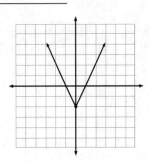

3. Dilate the parallelogram using a scale factor of 2.

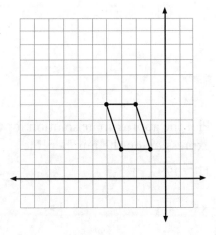

7. Is the relationship represented a function?

_____

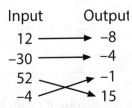

4. Are the triangles similar?

_____

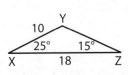

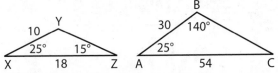

8. $(9.8 \times 10^3) - (3.1 \times 10^3) =$ _____

Spiral Review

Name: _____   Date: _____

Directions: Solve each problem.

1. Find the length of the line segment formed by connecting the two points.

$c =$ _____

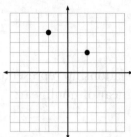

2. Solve the system of equations by graphing.

$y = -2x - 2$

$y = \frac{3}{2}x + 5$

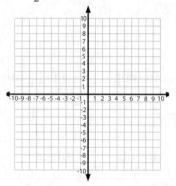

Solution: _____

3. Solve the inequality, and graph the solution on the number line.

$4(x - 3) + 2(x + 2) \le 22$

a. Solution: _____

b.

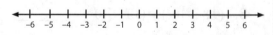

4. $\triangle JKL \sim \triangle MNO$

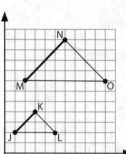

a. What is the slope of line MN?

_____

b. What is the slope of line JK?

_____

5. $5.6 \times 10^6 + 4.3 \times 10^6 =$ _____

6. Plot the approximate solution for the expression on the number line.

$11 - \sqrt{99}$

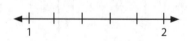

7. $\dfrac{x^4 y^5}{x^3 y^4} =$ _____

Spiral Review

Directions: Solve each problem.

1. Dilate the figure using a scale factor of $\frac{1}{4}$.

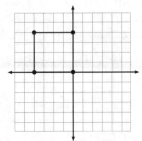

2. The graph shows Ling's savings over the last month.

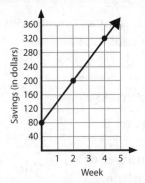

   a. How much money was in Ling's account at the start of the month?
_____

   b. How much money is Ling adding to his account each week? _____

   c. Write an equation to represent the situation.

     $y = $ _____

3. Solve the system of equations. Then, write whether there is one solution, no solution, or infinite solutions.

$y = 3x + 2$

$4y - 12x = 8$

   a. Solution: _____

   b. _____

4. Is the relationship represented below a function?

_____

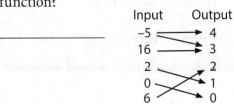

5. Write an equation for the line on the graph.

$y = $ _____

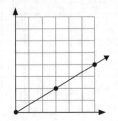

6. Does the relationship on the graph represent a proportional relationship?

_____

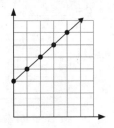

7. Plot the approximate locations of the numbers on the number line.

$\sqrt{58}, \sqrt{71}, \sqrt{65}$

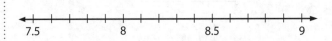

8. What is the measure of angle x?

$x = $ _____

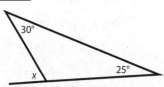

Name: _____ **Date:** _____

Directions: Solve each problem.

1. What scale factor was used to dilate rectangle *JKLM* to *J'K'L'M'*?

_____

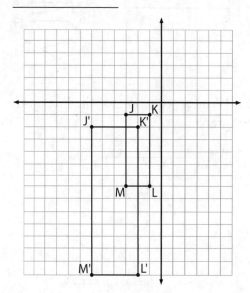

2. Find the length of the line segment formed by the two points.

$c =$ _____

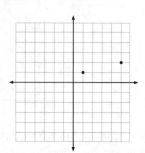

3. $5(x + 3) - 6(x - 2) + 3 = 3(x - 6)$

$x =$ _____

4. Is (2, 7) a solution to the system of equations?

$2x + y = 8$

$y = 4x - 1$

_____

5. What is the rate of change represented on the graph?

_____

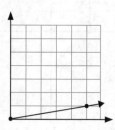

6. Which company offers a lower price per download?

_____

Company A: $y = 9x$

Company B:

Number of Downloads	Cost
10	$75
15	$112.50
20	$150

7. Write $0.\overline{17}$ as a fraction.

_____

8. $\frac{1}{4}(24 - 12) + 2.4 - \frac{4}{10} - (-8) =$ _____

Spiral Review

Learn about Scatterplots and Bivariate Data

A **scatterplot** uses dots on a graph to show a large amount of data.

Bivariate data are data that have two variables—the independent variable and the dependent variable. The independent variable is represented on the *x*-axis, while the dependent variable is represented on the *y*-axis.

Data on a scatterplot can be increasing, or have positive association. The data can also be decreasing, or have negative association. If the data are scattered with no pattern visible, there is no association with the data.

Data on a scatterplot can be linear or nonlinear. If the data appear to form a straight line, then the data have a linear association. If the data are curved or in any pattern that does not resemble a line, then the data have a nonlinear association.

Example 1

Do the data have positive association, negative association, or no association?

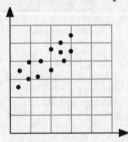

1. Do the data on the graph appear to be increasing or decreasing?

   _____

2. Because the data are increasing, they have positive association.

Example 2

Do the data on the scatterplot have a linear or nonlinear association?

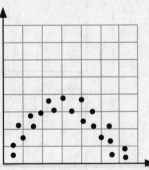

1. Are the data on the graph in the shape of a straight line?

   _____

2. Because the data appear to be curved, they have a nonlinear association.

Name: _____   Date: _____

☞ Quick Tip

To create a scatterplot, first identify the independent and dependent variables. Label the independent variable on the *x*-axis and the dependent variable on the *y*-axis. Determine a scale for each axis, and plot the data.

Directions: Construct a scatterplot for each table of data.

1. The table shows the number of hours different employees worked over 6 days.

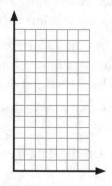

Day	1	1	1	2	2	3	3	3	4	4	4	5	5	6	6	6
Hours Worked	6	10	5	8	7	9	12	10	8	9	11	10	8	9	10	8

2. The table shows the total time different students studied to prepare for their math test along with their test score.

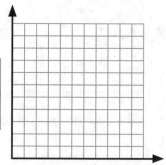

Time (minutes)	10	10	15	15	15	20	20	30	35	35	40	45	45	45	50	55
Test Score (percent)	58	63	65	65	70	72	78	65	80	78	85	85	92	95	91	100

3. The table shows the number of hot dogs sold at different stands at baseball games throughout the season.

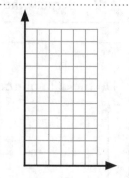

Stand Number	1	1	1	2	2	2	3	3	3	4	4	4	5	5	5	5
Number of Hot Dogs Sold	120	150	80	65	90	50	120	140	100	70	90	110	85	50	60	80

4. The table shows the number of apples picked by different groups throughout the week at the apple orchard.

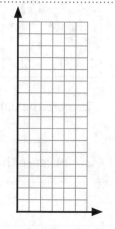

Day	1	1	1	1	2	2	2	3	3	3	4	4	4	4	5	5
Number of Apples Picked	90	250	20	150	50	55	90	200	180	80	90	220	80	50	150	180

Name: _____ **Date:** _____

Directions: Write whether each scatterplot has a positive association, negative association, or no association.

1. _____

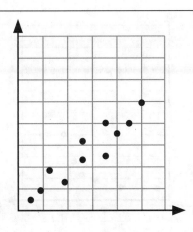

4. _____

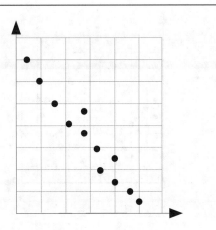

2. _____

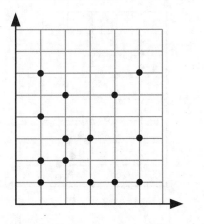

5. _____

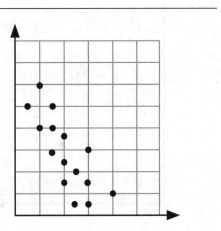

3. _____

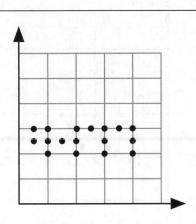

6. _____

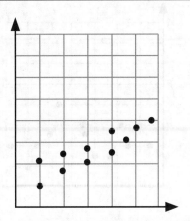

Scatterplots and Bivariate Data

Name: _____ Date: _____

Directions: Write whether each scatterplot shows a linear association or a nonlinear association.

1. _____

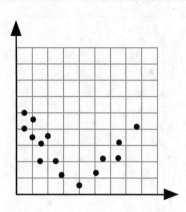

4. _____

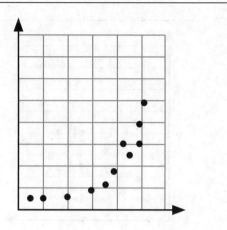

2. _____

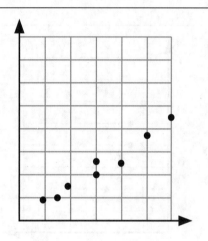

5. _____

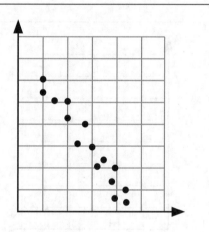

3. _____

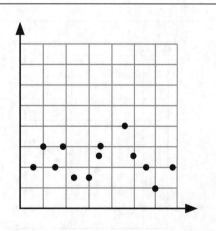

6. _____

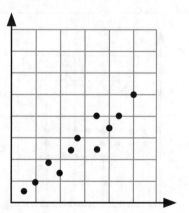

🖎 Quick Tip

If the data points are close together, you can say there is a strong association. If the data points are more spread out but are still in an increasing or decreasing pattern, you can say there is a weak association.

An **outlier** is a value in a data set that is very different from the rest of the data points.

A **cluster** is a group of data points that are very close together.

Directions: Circle whether there is a positive, negative, or no association for each graph. Then, complete the sentences, and answer the questions.

1.

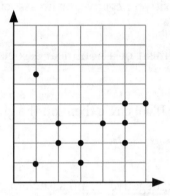

   a. positive   negative   none

   b. There is one _____ located above the rest of the data.

   c. Do the data have linear association? _____

3.

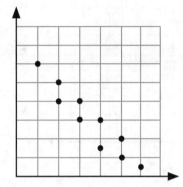

   a. positive   negative   none

   b. Are there any outliers? _____

   c. Do the data have linear association? _____

2.

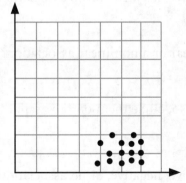

   a. positive   negative   none

   b. There is a _____ of data located above the *x*-axis.

   c. Do the data have linear association? _____

4.

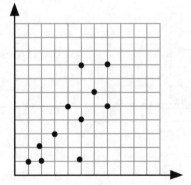

   a. positive   negative   none

   b. Is the association strong or weak? _____

   c. Are there any outliers? _____

Scatterplots and Bivariate Data

Name: _____   Date: _____

Directions: Solve each problem, and complete each task.

1. The table shows the number of years people were in a gardening club and the number of plants they planted last spring. Make a scatterplot of the data.

Number of Years	2	2	2	3	3	3	3	4	4	5	5	5	5	8	8	8	8	8	10	10
Number of Plants	8	10	6	12	15	6	16	20	22	28	25	21	18	21	25	24	18	15	25	27

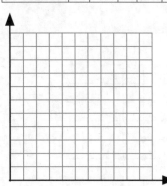

a. Does the graph have positive, negative, or no association?

_____

b. Does the graph have a linear or a nonlinear association?

_____

c. Are there any outliers? If so, circle them on the graph.

_____

2.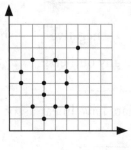

a. Does the graph have positive, negative, or no association?

_____

b. Does the graph have a linear or a nonlinear association?

_____

c. Are there any outliers? If so, circle them on the graph.

_____

3.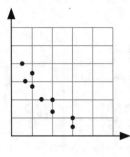

a. Does the graph have positive, negative, or no association?

_____

b. Does the graph have a linear or a nonlinear association?

_____

c. Are there any outliers? If so, circle them on the graph.

_____

4.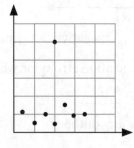

a. Does the graph have positive, negative, or no association?

_____

b. Does the graph have a linear or a nonlinear association?

_____

c. Are there any outliers? If so, circle them on the graph.

_____

Learn about Trend Lines

A **trend line** is a line drawn on a scatterplot that comes close to as many points as possible. It helps model the relationship between two variables. The line, or model, should have the same number of data points above and below the line. Some points can be on the line. Outliers should be ignored. You can write an equation to represent the line drawn and use the line and equation to make predictions.

Example

The graph shows how much rain fell in different locations over time during a thunderstorm. Draw a trend line on the scatterplot. Then, write an equation to represent the trend line.

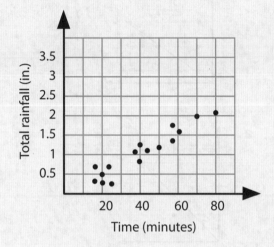

1. First, draw a trend line. Be sure the line has about the same number of points above and below the line.

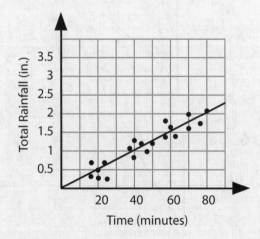

2. Write an equation for the trend line. Choose two points on the line, and find the slope of the line. Use (20, 0.5) and (80, 2). What is the slope of the line? _____

3. The y-intercept is 0, so now write the equation in slope-intercept form.

$y = mx + b$

$y =$ _____

Name: _____   Date: _____

Directions: Circle the graph that has the more accurate trend line for each pair of graphs.

1. a.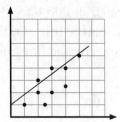

    b.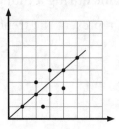

4. a.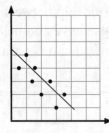

    b.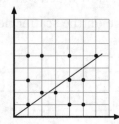

2. a.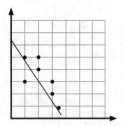

    b.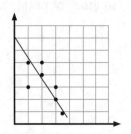

5. a.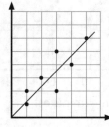

    b.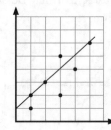

3. a.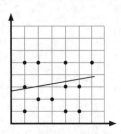

    b.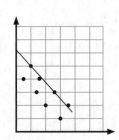

6. a.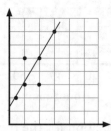

    b.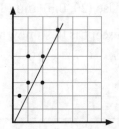

Name: _____ **Date:** _____

👆 Quick Tip

There should be about the same number of points above and below a trend line. The closer the points are to the line, the more accurate it is.

Directions: Draw a trend line on each graph.

1.

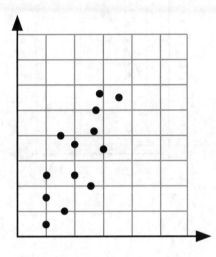

4.

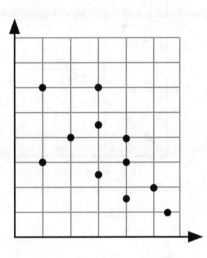

2.

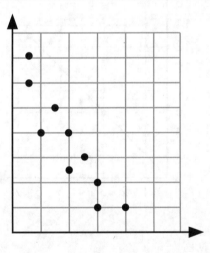

5.

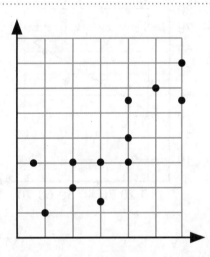

3.

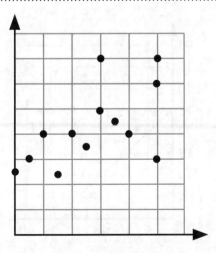

6.

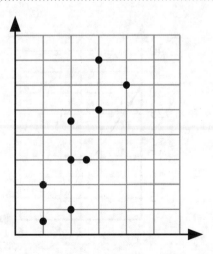

Trend Lines

Name: _____ **Date:** _____

Directions: Write an equation for the trend line drawn on each graph.

1. $y =$ _____

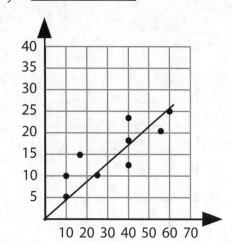

4. $y =$ _____

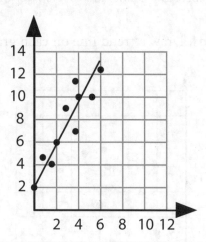

2. $y =$ _____

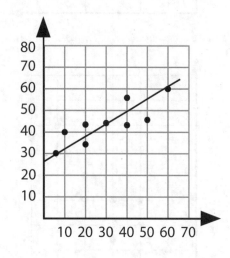

5. $y =$ _____

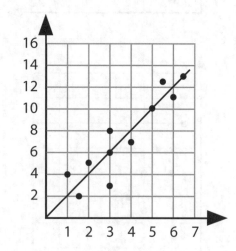

3. $y =$ _____

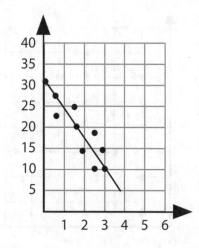

6. $y =$ _____

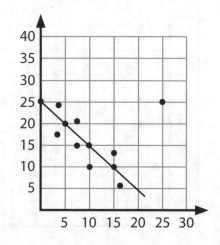

Trend Lines

Directions: For each pair of graphs, circle the one with the trend line that would give more accurate predictions.

1. **a.**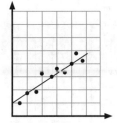

b.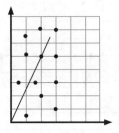

4. **a.**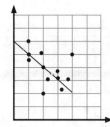

b.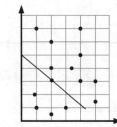

2. **a.**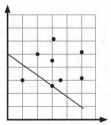

b.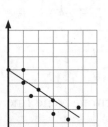

5. **a.**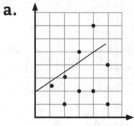

b.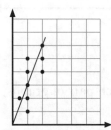

3. **a.**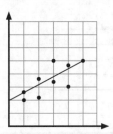

b.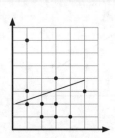

6. **a.**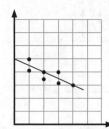

b.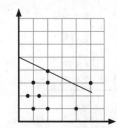

Trend Lines

Name: _____ **Date:** _____

Directions: Draw a trend line for each scatterplot. Write an equation to represent the line.

1. _y_ = _____

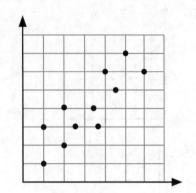

3. _y_ = _____

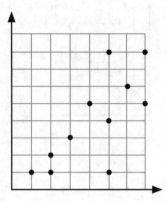

2. _y_ = _____

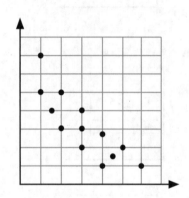

4. _y_ = _____

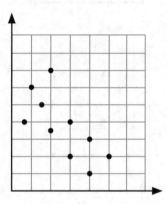

Directions: For each pair of graphs, circle the one with the more accurate trend line.

5. a.

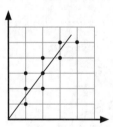

b.

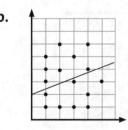

6. a.

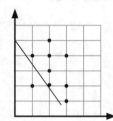

b.

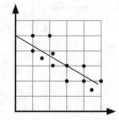

Trend Lines

Name: _____   **Date:** _____

Directions: Solve each problem.

1. The graph shows Jasmine's savings account over time.

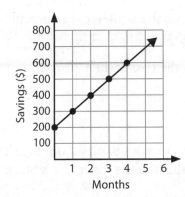

a. Does the line have negative or positive association? _____

b. What is the *y*-intercept? _____

c. What does the *y*-intercept represent in this situation? _____

d. What is the slope of the line? _____

e. What does the slope represent in this situation? _____

f. How much money will Jasmine have in her savings account after 1 year? _____

2. The graph shows the amount of money Everett spent at the mall over time.

a. Does the line have positive or negative association? _____

b. What is the *y*-intercept? _____

c. What does the *y*-intercept represent in this situation? _____

d. What is the slope of the line? _____

e. What does the slope represent in this situation? _____

f. If he continues at this rate, how much money will Everett spend if he spends 400 minutes at the mall? _____

3. The graph shows how the amount of time spent playing sports affects student grades.

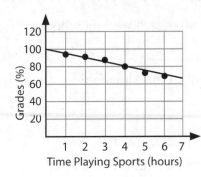

a. Does the line have negative or positive association? _____

b. What is the *y*-intercept? _____

c. What does the *y*-intercept represent in this situation? _____

d. What is the slope of the line? _____

e. What does the slope represent in this situation? _____

f. If a student plays sports for 5 hours, what is their expected grade? _____

Trend Lines

Name: _____ Date: _____

Trend Lines

Directions: Solve each problem.

1. A company is selling T-shirts, n. The cost of the shirts, C, is represented by the equation: $C = 8n + 25$.

   a. What is the slope? _____

   b. What does the slope represent in this situation? _____

   c. What is the y-intercept? _____

   d. What does the y-intercept represent in this situation? _____

   e. What is the cost of 20 T-shirts?

   _____

2. The equation $y = -20x + 200$ represents the amount of money in Darrah's bank account each week, where x represents the number of weeks and y represents the balance in Darrah's bank account.

   a. Is Darrah depositing or withdrawing money from her account? How do you know? _____

   b. What is the slope? _____

   c. What does the slope represent in this situation? _____

   d. What is the y-intercept? _____

   e. What does the y-intercept represent in this situation? _____

3. The graph shows the weight (in pounds) of strawberries (in pints).

   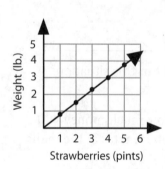

   a. What is the slope of the line? _____

   b. What does the slope represent in this situation?

   _____

   c. What is the y-intercept? _____

   d. What does the y-intercept represent in this situation?

   _____

   e. How much will 10 pints of strawberries weigh? _____

4. The graph shows the number of pencils Mrs. Jamison has left after each week of school.

   a. What is the slope? _____

   b. What does the slope represent in this situation?

   _____

   c. What is the y-intercept? _____

   d. What does the y-intercept represent in this situation?

   _____

   e. How many pencils will Mrs. Jamison have left after 5 weeks? _____

Name: _____ **Date:** _____

Directions: Complete the tasks, and answer the questions for each graph.

1. The scatterplot shows the distance walked by various people over time.

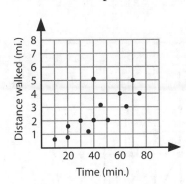

a. Draw a trend line to represent the relationship between time walked and distance walked.

b. Write an equation for the trend line. $y =$ _____

c. What does the slope represent in this situation?

_____

d. What does the y-intercept represent in this situation?

_____

2. The scatterplot shows the value of cell phones over time.

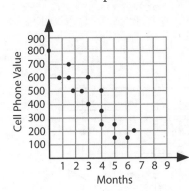

a. Draw a trend line to represent the relationship between months and cell phone value.

b. Write an equation for the trend line. $y =$ _____

c. What does the slope represent in this situation?

_____

d. What does the y-intercept represent in this situation?

_____

3. The scatterplot shows time studying and test scores.

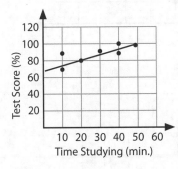

a. Write an equation for the trend line. $y =$ _____

b. What does the slope represent in this situation?

_____

c. What does the y-intercept represent in this situation?

_____

4. The graph shows a savings account balance over months.

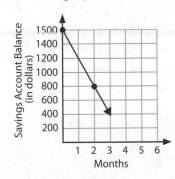

a. Write an equation for the trend line. $y =$ _____

b. What does the slope represent in this situation?

_____

c. What does the y-intercept represent in this situation?

_____

Trend Lines

Name: _____ **Date:** _____

Directions: The trend line drawn on each graph is not accurate. Draw a more appropriate line for each graph.

1.

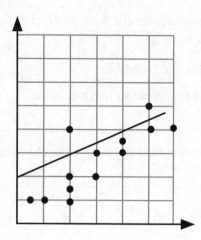

4.

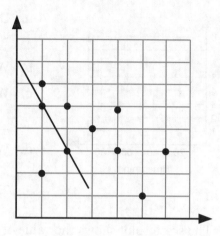

2.

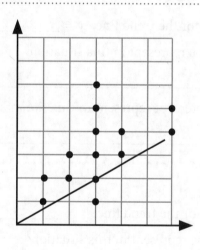

5.

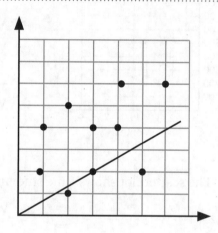

3.

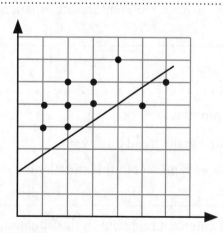

6.

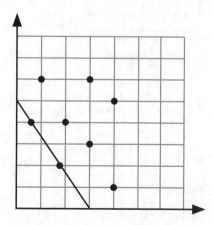

Trend Lines

142250—180 Days of Math

Name: _____   Date: _____

Directions: Identify the slope and *y*-intercept for each trend line. Then, use them to write the equation for the line.

1.

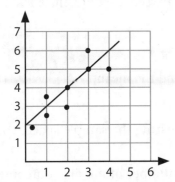

a. Slope: _____

b. *y*-intercept: _____

c. Equation: _____

4.

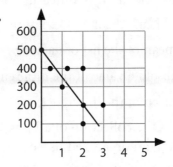

a. Slope: _____

b. *y*-intercept: _____

c. Equation: _____

2.

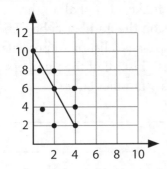

a. Slope: _____

b. *y*-intercept: _____

c. Equation: _____

5.

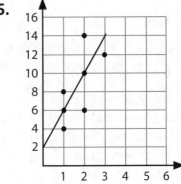

a. Slope: _____

b. *y*-intercept: _____

c. Equation: _____

3.

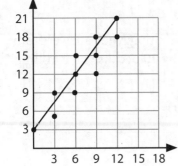

a. Slope: _____

b. *y*-intercept: _____

c. Equation: _____

6.

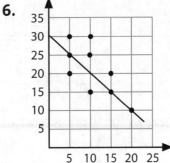

a. Slope: _____

b. *y*-intercept: _____

c. Equation: _____

Trend Lines

Learn about Variability and Probability

The **mean absolute deviation**, also referred to as the MAD, is the average distance between each data point and the mean. It is a measure of how spread out or dispersed a set of values is.

To calculate the Mean Absolute Deviation, follow these steps.

1. Find the mean of the list of data.

2. Find the absolute value of the difference of each data point and the mean.

3. Find the mean of the differences. This is the MAD.

A **sample space** is the collection of all possible outcomes. When listing the sample space, you can use a tree diagram, an organized list, or an area model.

Theoretical probability is the ratio of favorable outcomes to the number of possible outcomes.

Example 1

Find the Mean Absolute Deviation for the list of data.

1, 4, 4, 6, 6, 6, 8, 9, 10

1. Find the mean.

   $1 + 4 + 4 + 6 + 6 + 6 + 8 + 9 + 10 = 54$

   $54 \div 9 = 6$

2. Find the absolute value of the differences of each data point from the mean. How far away is each number from the mean you found in step 1? List the differences.

   $|1 - 6| = 5$

   $|4 - 6| = 2$

   $|4 - 6| = 2$

   $|6 - 6| = 0$

   $|6 - 6| = 0$

   $|6 - 6| = 0$

   $|8 - 6| = 2$

   $|9 - 6| = 3$

   $|10 - 6| = 4$

3. Find the mean of the the differences from step 2.

   $5 + 2 + 2 + 0 + 0 + 0 + 2 + 3 + 4 = 18$

   $18 \div 9 = 2$

Example 2

Find the sample space when you roll a fair, six-sided number cube.

1. You can make a list of all of the numbers on the number cube. The sample space is a list of all possible outcomes. List all of the numbers from a fair number cube.

   _____

   _____

Example 3

Dante rolls a standard number cube 20 times. How many times can he expect to roll a 6?

1. What is the theoretical probability of rolling a 6?

   1 out of 6

2. Next, multiply your answer from step 1 by 20 because he is rolling 20 times.

   $\frac{1}{6} \times 20 = $ _____

🖎 Quick Tip

To find the mean of a list of data, add all of the data points together to find the sum. Then, divide the sum by the total number of data points. The answer is the mean.

Directions: Find the mean and the Mean Absolute Deviation (MAD) of each set of data.

1. 20, 25, 32, 40, 48

    a. Mean: _____

    b. MAD: _____

2. 115, 155, 180, 191, 209, 245, 305

    a. Mean: _____

    b. MAD: _____

3. 15.6, 22.8, 25.4, 27.2, 30, 45, 50.5, 67.5

    a. Mean: _____

    b. MAD: _____

4. 225, 278, 300, 340, 422, 575, 660

    a. Mean: _____

    b. MAD: _____

5. 15, 26, 31, 44, 53, 67, 70, 85, 90, 99

    a. Mean: _____

    b. MAD: _____

6. 231, 301, 332, 405, 447, 478, 556, 682

    a. Mean: _____

    b. MAD: _____

7. 51, 53, 55, 57, 68, 71, 75, 98

    a. Mean: _____

    b. MAD: _____

8. 37, 38, 49, 87, 95, 110, 112, 120

    a. Mean: _____

    b. MAD: _____

9. 21, 36, 36, 38, 45, 46, 58, 88

    a. Mean: _____

    b. MAD: _____

10. 111, 115, 132, 166, 188, 206, 266, 304

    a. Mean: _____

    b. MAD: _____

Variability and Probability

Name: _____ Date: _____

Directions: List the sample space for each question. The first one has been modeled for you.

1. You flip two fair coins.
   Sample Space: heads/heads, heads/tails,
   tails/heads, tails/tails

2. You spin the spinner.

   Sample Space: _____
   _____

3. You choose a block from a bag with 4 blue blocks and 1 red block.

   Sample Space: _____
   _____

4. You roll a number cube and then flip a coin.

   Sample Space: _____
   _____

5. You toss a coin 3 times.

   Sample Space: _____
   _____

6. You roll a 12-sided number cube. Each number appears once on the number cube.

   Sample Space: _____
   _____

7. You spin a spinner with equal pieces numbered 1 through 10.

   Sample Space: _____
   _____

   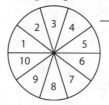

8. You are drawing a winner from a table of 6 students to win a homework pass.

   Sample Space: _____
   _____

9. You put the letters from the word *MATH* in a bag and draw one letter without looking.

   Sample Space: _____
   _____

10. Pieces of paper with numbers 1–10 written on them are thrown in a hat. You choose one of the pieces of paper.

    Sample Space: _____
    _____

Name: _____ **Date:** _____

> ### ✎ Quick Tip
>
> A **random sample** is the most reliable sample because every event has the same chance of occurring. Random samples are unbiased.

Directions: Determine whether each sample will be a random sample. Write *Random* or *Not Random*. If it is not a random sample, explain why not.

1. Maxine, an 8th grader, wants to know what 8th graders do in their free time after school. She decides to ask students in her first period class.

   _____

2. Sifa wants to know what the most popular smoothie flavor is at the Smoothie Shop. He surveys every 5th customer who enters the shop for 2 weeks.

   _____

3. The package delivery company wants to know, on average, what time the packages are delivered by their drivers. They decide to ask the people who live on the same street as the delivery company.

   _____

4. The student council at the middle school wants to know what students would like to do for homecoming. They decide to put together a survey and pass it out to 5 students in every homeroom who were chosen through a lottery by the teacher.

   _____

5. The principal of the middle school wants to choose 25 students to attend an honors band competition. He chooses 25 students with the highest grade point average.

   _____

6. Mr. Sever wants to choose five 8th grade student aides for the kindergarten class. She places all the student identification numbers on slips of paper into a hat, and chooses 5 numbers. Those students become the student aides in the kindergarten class.

   _____

7. A streaming service wants to know what types of programs are most popular to viewers. They decide to survey 50 people at the grocery store on Sunday morning.

   _____

8. The math teacher wants to know about how many minutes students spend studying for their math test. She assigns each student in 8th grade a number and uses a number generator program to select 40 numbers. These are the students she collects data from.

   _____

Name: _____ Date: _____

Directions: Solve each problem.

1. A six-sided number cube is rolled.

    a. What is the probability of rolling a 3? _____

    b. What is the probability of rolling a prime number? _____

    c. What is the probability of rolling an even number? _____

2. A spinner is spun.

    a. What is the probability of spinning an 8? _____

    b. What is the probability of spinning a factor of 8? _____

    c. What is the probability of spinning a factor of 5? _____

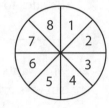

3. Two coins are flipped.

    a. What is the probability that two heads are flipped? _____

    b. What is the probability that at least one coin is tails? _____

    c. What is the probability that one coin is heads and one coin is tails? _____

4. A spinner is spun two times and the outcomes are added together.

    a. What is the probability that the sum of the two spins is 8? _____

    b. What is the probability that the sum of the two spins is an even number? _____

    c. What is the probability that the sum of the two spins is greater than 6? _____

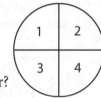

5. A spinner is spun.

    a. What is the probability of spinning a prime number? _____

    b. What is the probability of spinning a number greater than 2? _____

    c. What is the probability of spinning a factor of 4? _____

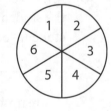

6. A marble is chosen from a bag with 5 blue marbles, 3 green marbles, and 2 red marbles.

    a. What is the probability of drawing a blue marble? _____

    b. What is the probability of drawing a red marble? _____

    c. What is the probability of drawing a yellow marble? _____

Name: _____ **Date:** _____

Directions: Solve each problem. Show your work.

1. If Marco rolls a fair number cube 600 times, how many times can he expect to roll a 5?

_____

2. If Justice spins the spinner 200 times, how many times can she expect to spin the letter A?

_____

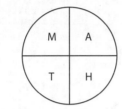

3. If Yaneli flips a fair coin 150 times, how many times can she expect to flip heads?

_____

4. Sadie is flipping a coin 3 times. She finds the theoretical probability of flipping all 3 heads as $\frac{1}{8}$. If she performs the experiment 200 times (600 total flips), about how many times can she expect to flip all heads?

_____

5. Dareon is choosing a card from a standard deck. What is the probability that he will choose a card that is hearts?

_____

6. Cameron is rolling a standard number cube 300 times. How many times can he expect to roll a factor of 5?

_____

7. Frederick is choosing a card from a standard deck. What is the probability that he will choose a card that is a king?

_____

8. Hector chooses a block 100 times from a bag with 8 blue blocks and 2 green blocks, replacing his block each time. How many times can he expect to choose a green block?

_____

9. Stevie spins the spinner 60 times to determine her lunch. How many times can she expect to spin ham?

_____

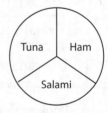

10. Ginny chooses a marble 250 times from a bag with 3 red marbles and 2 black marbles. How many times can Ginny expect to choose a black marble?

_____

Learn about Two-Way Tables

A **two-way frequency table** is a way to display frequencies for two different categories from a single group.

A **frequency** tells us how many times a data value occurs.

A **relative frequency** is the ratio of the actual number of favorable events to the total possible number of events. Relative frequencies can be written as fractions, decimals, or percents.

Example

A restaurant surveyed their customers on their favorite dish. The results are shown in the table.

	Male	Female	Total
steak	75	50	**125**
chicken	60	95	**155**
total	**135**	**145**	**280**

Find the relative frequencies as percents.

1. Relative frequencies can be written as row totals. Write the missing percents.

	Male	Female	Total
steak	$\frac{75}{125} = $ _____ %	$\frac{50}{125} = $ _____ %	$\frac{125}{125} = $ _____ %
chicken	$\frac{60}{155} = $ _____ %	$\frac{95}{155} = $ _____ %	$\frac{155}{155} = $ _____ %
total	$\frac{135}{280} = $ _____ %	$\frac{145}{280} = $ _____ %	$\frac{280}{280} = $ _____ %

2. Relative frequencies can be written as column totals. Write the missing percents.

	Male	Female	Total
steak	$\frac{75}{135} = $ _____ %	$\frac{50}{145} = $ _____ %	$\frac{125}{280} = $ _____ %
chicken	$\frac{60}{135} = $ _____ %	$\frac{95}{145} = $ _____ %	$\frac{155}{280} = $ _____ %
total	$\frac{135}{135} = $ _____ %	$\frac{145}{145} = $ _____ %	$\frac{280}{280} = $ _____ %

3. You can answer questions based on the results of the relative frequencies. For example, what percent of all people surveyed prefer chicken?

   Look at the results of the columns. The total number of people who preferred chicken was 155. There was a total of 280 people surveyed. What is the percent of people surveyed who prefer chicken?
   $\frac{155}{280} = 55.36\%$

Name: _____ Date: _____

Directions: Read each scenario. Complete the two-way table to organize the data.

1. All of the 7th and 8th graders voted on their favorite lunch foods.

   - Out of the 8th graders, 84 voted for pizza, 36 voted for hamburger, and 12 voted for salad.

   - Out of the 7th graders, 78 voted for pizza, 29 voted for hamburger, and 8 voted for salad.

	7th Graders	8th Graders
pizza		
hamburger		
salad		
total		

2. The 8th grade class held an election for two candidates running for student council president.

   - Candidate A was voted for by 14 girls and 11 boys.

   - Candidate B was voted for by 6 girls and 3 boys.

	Girls	Boys
candidate A		
candidate B		
total		

3. Mr. Mendez asked his students how many of them have a dog and how many have a cat.

   - Out of the 7th graders, 12 said they have a dog and 9 said they have a cat.

   - Out of the 8th graders, 9 said they have a dog and 5 said they have a cat.

	7th Graders	8th Graders
dog		
cat		
total		

4. Tyrese asked his friends what music they liked to listen to.

   - Rock was chosen by 12 twelve-year-old friends and 15 thirteen-year-old friends.

   - Country was chosen by 9 twelve-year-old friends and 4 thirteen-year-old friends.

   - Rap was chosen by 8 twelve-year-old friends and 3 thirteen-year-old friends.

	12-Year-Old Friends	13-Year-Old Friends
rock		
country		
rap		
total		

Two-Way Tables

Name: _____ Date: _____

Directions: Complete each table, and answer the questions.

1. Students were given two color choices to choose from for their art project. The results are in the table.

	Boys	Girls	Total
red	11	13	
blue	19	17	
total			

   a. What percent of the students who chose red are girls? _____

   b. What fraction of total boys chose red? _____

   c. What percent of the students surveyed were girls? _____

   d. What percent of the boys chose blue? _____

2. Students were required to email their assignments to the teacher. The teacher recorded the emails she received in a two-way table.

	Male	Female
sent email	15	12
did not send email	3	2
total		

   a. What fraction of the emails received came from male students? _____

   b. What was the total number of emails sent by all students? _____

   c. What percent of the female students did not send the email? _____

   d. What percent of all of the students were male? _____

3. A home improvement store is considering a promotion. They want to know if customers of different age groups would be interested in a free gallon of paint if offered with any purchase over $20. The results are recorded in the table.

	Yes	No
ages 18–25	60	20
ages 26–40	35	10
ages 41–60	40	55
total		

   a. What percent of the interested customers are from the 18–25 group? _____

   b. What percent of the total people surveyed answered *yes*? _____

   c. What fraction of the surveyed people were ages 26–40? _____

   d. What percent of the 26–40 age group said *no*, they would not be interested? _____

✎ Quick Tip

When comparing data using relative frequencies in a two-way table, you can compare them by column or by row.

Directions: Find the relative frequencies of the two-way tables. Round percents to the nearest hundredth, if needed.

Adults and teens were asked what they prefer to drink while exercising. The results are shown in the table.

	Teens	Adults	Total
sports drink	80	30	110
water	50	75	125
total	130	105	235

1. Calculate the relative frequencies by row.

	Teens	Adults	Total
sports drink			
water			
total			

2. Calculate the relative frequencies by column.

	Teens	Adults	Total
sports drink			
water			
total			

The cafeteria workers wanted to know how many students buy lunch and how many pack lunch. The results are shown in the table.

	Boys	Girls	Total
buy lunch	68	34	102
pack lunch	24	42	66
total	92	76	168

3. Calculate the relative frequencies by row.

	Boys	Girls	Total
buy lunch			
pack lunch			
total			

4. Calculate the relative frequencies by column.

	Boys	Girls	Total
buy lunch			
pack lunch			
total			

Two-Way Tables

Name: _____   Date: _____

Directions: Answer the questions about each set of data.

Two-Way Tables

1. An auto dealership is keeping track of the most popular color and make of vehicle customers are buying. The results are shown in the table.

	Sedan	SUV	Total
black	50	90	140
white	45	85	130
total	95	175	270

   a. What percent of the total vehicles sold were black? _____

   b. What percent of the black vehicles sold were sedans? _____

   c. What percent of the total sedans sold were white? _____

   d. What percent of the white vehicles sold were SUVs? _____

2. A teacher surveyed students and asked if they preferred hard copies of books or digital copies. The results are shown in the table.

	7th Graders	8th Graders	Total
hard copies	43	57	100
digital copies	29	71	100
total	72	128	200

   a. What percent of 7th graders prefer digital copies? _____

   b. What percent of those who prefer hard copies are 8th graders?

   _____

   c. What percent of 8th graders prefer digital copies? _____

   d. What percent of those who prefer digital copies are 7th graders?

   _____

3. Theo wanted to know if students prefer bowling or laser tag. The results are shown in the table.

	Boys	Girls	Total
bowling	15	32	47
laser tag	40	18	58
total	55	50	105

   a. What percent of all students chose laser tag? _____

   b. What percent of boys chose bowling? _____

   c. What percent of those who chose laser tag are boys? _____

   d. What percent of girls chose laser tag? _____

4. Students were asked what season they prefer. The results are shown in the table.

	Boys	Girls	Total
spring	8	10	18
summer	20	25	45
fall	5	7	12
winter	6	8	14
total	39	50	89

   a. What percent of girls chose summer? _____

   b. What percent of all students chose winter? _____

   c. What percent of boys chose fall? _____

   d. What percent of all students chose spring? _____

Directions: Complete the tasks, and answer the questions.

1. Use the information to complete the two-way table.

   • Of the 125 students in sports/clubs, 75 are male.

   • Of the 40 students who have a part-time job, 30 are female.

   • Of the 80 students in band/chorus, 65 are female.

	Have a Part-Time Job	Sports/Clubs	Band/Chorus	Total
male				
female				
total				

2. Complete the relative frequency table using percents (rounded to the nearest tenth of a percent).

	Have a Part-Time Job	Sports/Clubs	Band/Chorus	Total
male				
female				
total				

3. What relative frequency of those who have a part-time job are female? _____

4. What relative frequency of the total males are in sports/clubs? _____

5. What relative frequency of the total females are in band/chorus? _____

6. What relative frequency of those who are in band/chorus are male? _____

. . . .

7. Use the information to complete the two-way table.

   • Of the 45 students who walk to school, 32 are 7th graders.

   • Of the 120 students who ride the bus, 90 are 8th graders.

   • Of the 50 students who get dropped off, 40 are 7th graders.

	Walk	Ride Bus	Dropped Off	Total
7th grade				
8th grade				
total				

8. Complete the relative frequency table using percents (rounded to the nearest tenth of a percent).

	Walk	Ride Bus	Dropped Off	Total
7th grade				
8th grade				
total				

9. What relative frequency of those who walk are 7th graders? _____

10. What relative frequency of all 7th graders ride the bus? _____

11. What relative frequency of all 8th graders are dropped off? _____

12. What relative frequency of those who ride the bus are 8th graders? _____

Two-Way Tables

Name: _____ Date: _____

Directions: Solve each problem.

1. Write $0.\overline{92}$ as a fraction.

_____

2. $\dfrac{3x^5y^6}{9x^3y^4} =$ _____

3. Write $\dfrac{17}{5}$ as a decimal. _____

4. $(\frac{3}{4})^2 \cdot 32 + 3(9 - 4) - 5^2 =$ _____

5. Order from least to greatest.

$-13\frac{3}{5}$, -13.9, $\frac{-130}{10}$, $-13\frac{1}{6}$

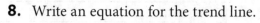

6. What two integers is $\sqrt{46}$ between?

_____ and _____

7. $x^2 = 81$

$x =$ _____

8. Write an equation for the trend line.

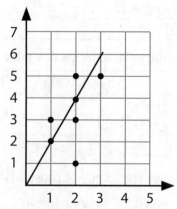

$y =$ _____

Directions: Solve each problem.

1. Estimate the value of the expression to the nearest tenth.

$9 + \sqrt{6} =$ _____

2. Does the relationship represented show a function?

_____

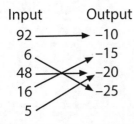

Input	Output
92	−10
6	−15
48	−20
16	−25
5	

3. Match the location of each number on the number line.

$\sqrt{95}, 8\frac{7}{8}, \sqrt{67}$

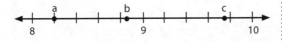

a. _____

b. _____

c. _____

4. Does the relationship on the graph show a function?

_____

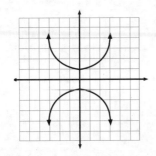

5. $(6.5 \times 10^3) - (3.3 \times 10^3) =$ _____

6. $15^2 =$ _____

7. Solve for x.

$2(x - 5) = 40$

$x =$ _____

8. What is the measure of angle x?

_____

16°

11° x

Cumulative Review

Name: _____ **Date:** _____

Directions: Solve each problem. Use the diagram to answer questions.

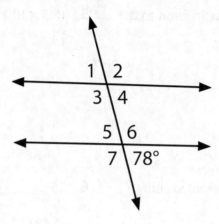

1. Name one pair of corresponding angles. _____

2. Name one pair of vertical angles. _____

3. What is the measure of angle 7? _____

4. What is the measure of angle 1? _____

5. Name one pair of supplementary angles. _____

6. What is the measure of angle 5? _____

7. Together, what type of angles are angles 5 and 6? _____

8. What is the sum of angles 1, 2, 3, and 4? _____

Name: _____   **Date:** _____

Directions: Solve each problem.

1. Use the graph to answer the questions.

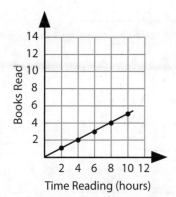

   a. Slope: _____

   b. y-intercept: _____

   c. Equation: _____

2. What is the measure of angle x?

_____

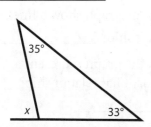

3. What transformations move figure 1 to figure 2?

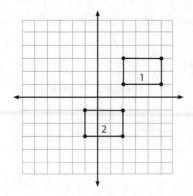

_____ and _____

4. What is the volume of the figure?

$V = $ _____

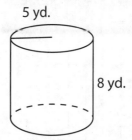

5. Does the relationship on the graph show a linear relationship?

_____

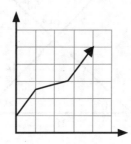

6. $\dfrac{(8.4 \times 10^7)}{(4.2 \times 10^5)} = $ _____

7. $11^2 = $ _____

8. $4(x - 6) + 3x = 2(x - 6)$

$x = $ _____

Cumulative Review

Name: _____ Date: _____

Directions: Solve each problem.

1. Does the relationship on the scatterplot have a positive association, negative association, or no association?

_____

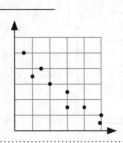

2. Is △ *ABE* similar to △ *DCE*?

_____

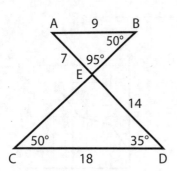

3. Write $2.\overline{4}$ as a mixed number.

_____

4. Does the table represent a linear function?

_____

x	y
−5	−2
0	3
5	8
10	13

5. What is the volume of the figure?

$V =$ _____

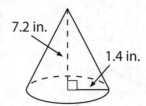

6. Use the graph to answer the questions.

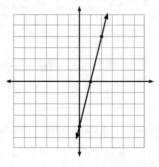

a. Does the graph show a linear relationship? _____

b. Does the graph represent a proportional relationship?

_____

7. $4[-3(9 - 7)^2 + 6] =$ _____

8. Order from least to greatest.

$\sqrt{15}, 3.1, \frac{18}{6}, \sqrt{24}$

_____

Name: _____ **Date:** _____

Directions: Solve each problem.

1. Two friends are making mugs. Which friend makes mugs faster?

_____

Leo: $y = 2.75x$

Mario:

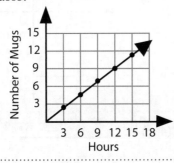

2. Which function has a greater slope?

_____

Function A: $y = -2x + 5$

Function B:

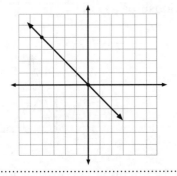

3. $(4x^3)^2 = $ _____

4. What is the volume of the figure?

$V = $ _____

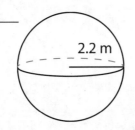

2.2 m

5. Does the system of equations have one solution, no solution, or infinite solutions?

_____

$2x + y = 14$

$-2x - y = 15$

6. Write an equation to represent the trend line.

$y = $ _____

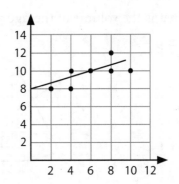

7. Compare using <, >, or =.

9.3 _____ $\sqrt{78}$

8. $\dfrac{10^7}{10^5} = $ _____

Cumulative Review

Name: _____ **Date:** _____

Directions: Solve each problem.

1. Does the relationship represented show a function?

_____

Input		Output
3	→	−4
7	→	2
8		6
3		9

2. Is $\sqrt{51}$ rational or irrational?

_____

3. What is the volume of the figure?

$V =$ _____

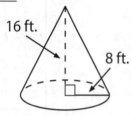

16 ft.

8 ft.

4. Use the graph to answer the questions.

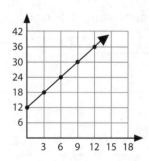

a. Does the graph represent a proportional relationship?

_____

b. What is the rate of change represented on the graph?

_____

5. Solve the system of equations by graphing.

$y = \frac{-7}{2}x - 4$

$y - x = 5$

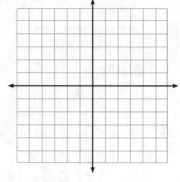

6. $(2x^3)(4x^4) =$ _____

7. Does the graph show a proportional relationship?

_____

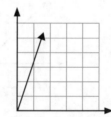

8. Which function has a greater y-intercept?

_____

Function A: $y = 3x + 3$

Function B:

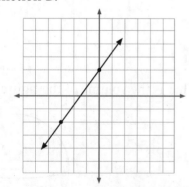

Cumulative Review

Name: _____   Date: _____

Directions: Solve each problem.

1. Does the relationship on the graph show a linear or nonlinear pattern?

_____

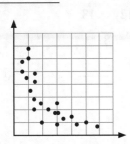

2. $\dfrac{(4.2 \times 10^8)}{(2.1 \times 10^6)} =$ _____

3. Is $\triangle DEC$ similar to $\triangle BAC$?

_____

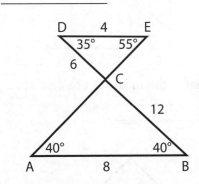

4. Is (1, 5) a solution to the system of equations?

_____

$y = 3x + 2$

$y - x = 4$

5. What is the volume of the figure?

$V =$ _____

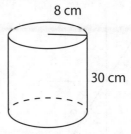

6. Plot the approximate value of $2\sqrt{8}$ on the number line.

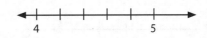

7. Is the relationship represented on the graph a function?

_____

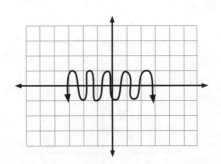

8. Which function has a smaller y-intercept?

_____

Function X: $y = -6x - 2$
Function Y:

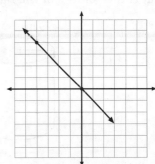

Cumulative Review

Name: _____ **Date:** _____

Directions: Solve each problem.

1. Write an equation for the line on the graph.

   $y =$ _____

   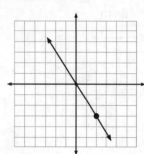

2. Plot the approximate value of $13 - \sqrt{79}$ on the number line.

   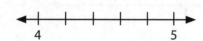

3. What transformations moved figure 1 to figure 2?

   _____ and _____

   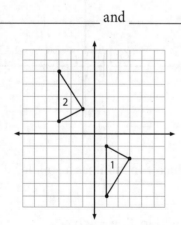

4. What is the volume of the figure?

   _____

   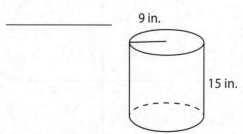
   9 in.

   15 in.

5. Does the system of equations have one solution, no solution, or infinite solutions?

   $18x + 12y = 48$

   $3x + 2y = 8$

   _____

6. Does the relationship on the graph represent a proportional relationship?

   _____

   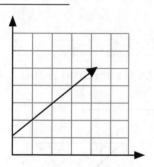

7. What is the measure of angle x?

   _____

   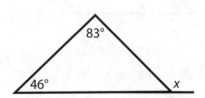
   83°
   46°   x

8. $\sqrt{49} =$ _____

Directions: Solve each problem.

1. Is Δ *FGH* similar to Δ *FJK*? _____

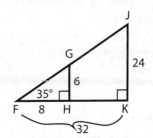

2. What is the cost per song according to the graph? _____

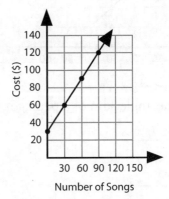

3. Plot the approximate location of each number on the number line.

$\sqrt{88}$, $\sqrt{76}$, $\sqrt{95}$

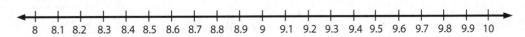

4. What transformation is shown on the graph? _____

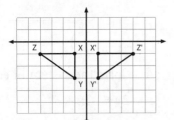

5. $\sqrt{121}$ = _____

6. Write an equation for the trend line shown on the graph.

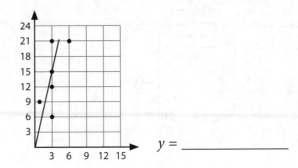

$y =$ _____

7. $5(8 - 12)^2 + 3 - 8(11 - 9)$ = _____

8. $x^2 = 49$

$x =$ _____

Name: _____   Date: _____

Directions: Solve each problem.

1. Sweaters are on sale at two stores. Which store has the lower price per sweater?

Sweaters R Us:

Number of Sweaters	Cost
5	$74.95
7	$104.93
9	$134.91
11	$164.89

Clothing Outfitters: $y = 15.25x$

_____

2. Does the relationship represented on the graph show a function?

_____

```
        Input      Output
         -3  ──────►  6
          6  ──────►  7
          5          8
          7  ──────►  9
          4          10
```

3. Is $\sqrt{5}$ rational or irrational?

_____

4. Solve the system of equations by graphing.

$2y = -2x + 6$

$y = 2x + 3$

Solution: _____

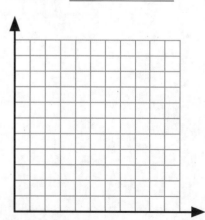

5. Write an equation for the trend line shown on the graph.

$y =$ _____

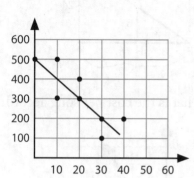

6. What is the angle sum of a pentagon?

_____

7. Which is larger: $\sqrt{9}$ or 9.4?

_____

8. What is the volume of the figure?

$V =$ _____

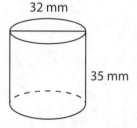

32 mm

35 mm

Directions: Solve each problem.

1. Does the relationship on the graph show a linear or nonlinear pattern? _____

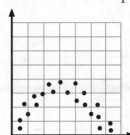

2. Plot the approximate location of each number on the number line.

$\sqrt{8}$, $\sqrt{17}$, $\sqrt{11}$

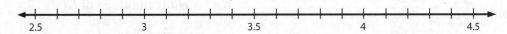

3. Does the relationship represented on the graph show a function?

_____

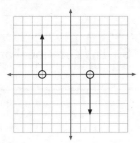

4. What is the volume of the figure?

$V =$ _____

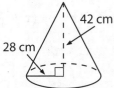

5. Does the system of equations have one solution, no solution, or infinite solutions?

_____

$y = -5x + 7$

$10x + 2y = 19$

6. What is the measure of angle x?

_____

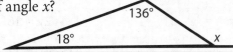

7. $y = -6x - 4$

    a. What is the slope? _____

    b. What is the y-intercept? _____

8. $(2.8 \times 10^3) + (5.1 \times 10^3) =$ _____

Name: _____ **Date:** _____

Directions: Solve each problem.

1. Is Δ *MNP* similar to Δ *JKL*?

_____

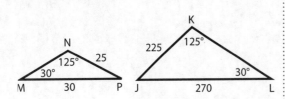

2. What is the rate of change represented on the graph?

_____

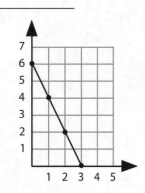

3. Find the measure of the missing side.

_____

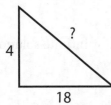
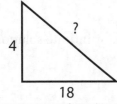

4. Dilate the figure using a scale factor of 2.

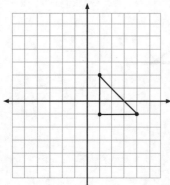

5. Δ *MNO* ~ Δ *XYZ*

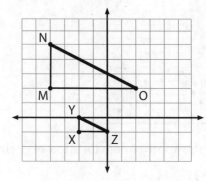

    a. What is the slope of *NO*?

    _____

    b. What is the slope of *YZ*?

    _____

6. Is $\sqrt{13}$ rational or irrational?

_____

7. $(x^4 y^5) \cdot (x^2 y^7) =$ _____

8. Solve the system of equations algebraically.

$4x - 2y = 16$

$4x - 4y = 12$

Solution: (_____, _____)

Directions: Solve each problem.

1. The graph shows the cost of a gym membership per month.

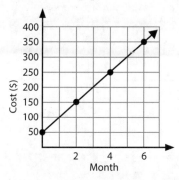

   a. Does the graph represent a proportional relationship?

   _____

   b. What is the cost of the membership per month?

   _____

2. Is △ *MNO* similar to △ *PQR*?

   _____

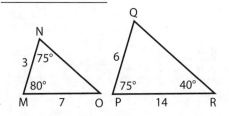

3. Does the system of equations have one solution, no solution, or infinite solutions?

   $y = 5x$

   $4y = 20x - 16$

   _____

4. Does the graph represent a proportional relationship?

   _____

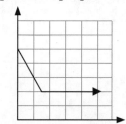

5. Write an equation to represent the line.

   $y =$ _____

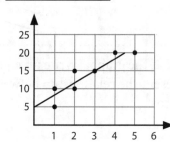

6. Write an equation for the trend line.

   $y =$ _____

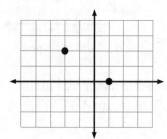

7. Find the distance between the two points on the graph.

   $c =$ _____

8. $-4(9 - 11) - 5^2 + 2^3 =$ _____

Name: _____   **Date:** _____

Directions: Solve each problem.

1. Does the relationship on the graph represent a proportional relationship?

_____

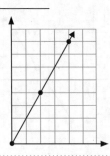

2. Does the relationship represented show a function?

_____

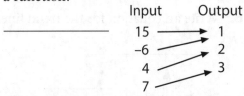

3. Look at the graph. Write an equation to represent the relationship between pears and cost.

$y =$ _____

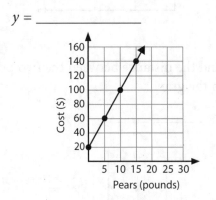

4. What scale factor was used to dilate figure *ABCD* to figure *A'B'C'D'*?

_____

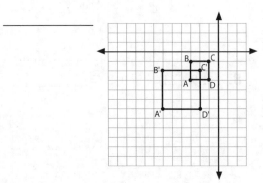

5. Is (–4, 4) a solution to the system of equations?

$y - 6 = \frac{1}{2}x$

$y = -x$

_____

6. Does the graph represent a linear function?

_____

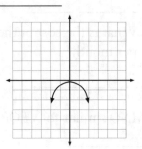

7. $\dfrac{g^4 h^5}{g^2 h^3} =$ _____

8. Is $\frac{29}{3}$ rational or irrational?

_____

Directions: Solve each problem.

1. Use the graph to answer the questions.

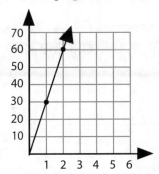

   a. Does the graph represent a proportional relationship?

_____

   b. What is the rate of change?

_____

2. Write a scenario to go with the graph.

_____

_____

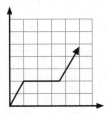

3. Is △ MLK similar to △ IHJ?

_____

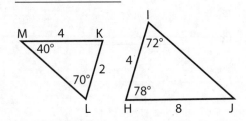

4. Is (2, 5) a solution to the system of equations?

$\frac{1}{2}x + y = 6$

$4x - y = 3$

_____

5. Does the graph shown represent a function?

_____

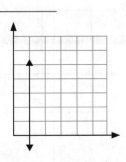

6. Find the distance between the two points on the graph.

$c =$ _____

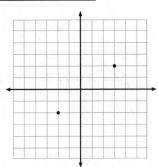

7. $\dfrac{(9.3 \times 10^4)}{(3.1 \times 10^2)} =$ _____

8. Solve the inequality, and graph the solution on the number line.

$8(x - 3) \le 8$

   a. Solution: _____

   b.

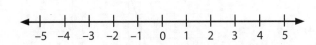

Cumulative Review

Name: _____   Date: _____

Directions: Solve each problem.

1. Dilate the figure using a scale factor of $\frac{1}{4}$.

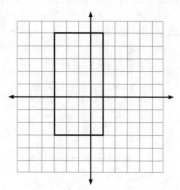

2. What is the missing side length?

_____

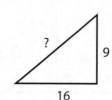

3. What is the volume of the figure?

_____

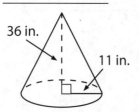

36 in.

11 in.

4. Is the graph linear or nonlinear?

_____

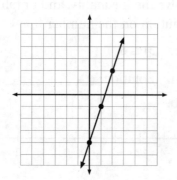

5. Which graph has the greater slope?

_____

Graph A   Graph B

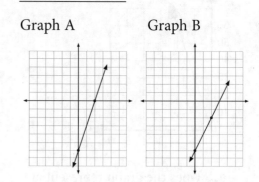

6. Does the graph represent a function?

_____

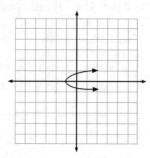

7. $x^2 = 225$

$x =$ _____

8. $(x^3 y^2)^2 =$ _____

Directions: Solve each problem.

1. $y = 4x + 7$

    a. Slope: _____

    b. y-intercept: _____

5. What is the volume of the figure?

$V =$ _____

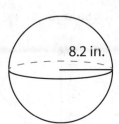

8.2 in.

2. Does the relationship represented on the graph show a function?

_____

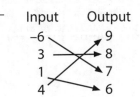

Input   Output
-6   9
3   8
1   7
4   6

6. Is the graph linear or nonlinear?

_____

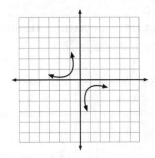

3. $\triangle ABC \sim \triangle DEF$

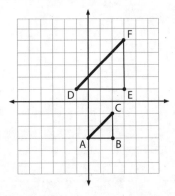

    a. What is the slope of AC?

    _____

    b. What is the slope of DF?

    _____

7. $\sqrt{144} - 3(5^2 - 3^2) =$ _____

8. Does the relationship on the graph represent a proportional relationship?

_____

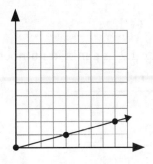

4. Find the missing side of the triangle.

$c =$ _____

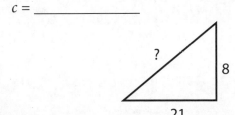

?   8
21

Cumulative Review

Name: _____ **Date:** _____

Directions: Solve each problem.

Cumulative Review

1. Which store is selling socks at a lower price per pair?

   Store A: Store B

x	y
2	$13
4	$26
6	$39
8	$52

   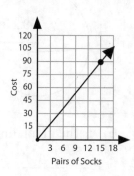

   Pairs of Socks

5. $\dfrac{12^4}{12^2} =$ _____

2. What transformations occurred to move shape 1 to shape 2?

   _____ and _____

   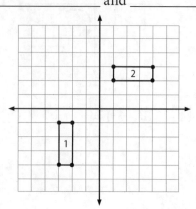

6. $-9(-6 - 8)^2 + (-4)^2 =$ _____

3. $x^3 = 343$

   $x =$ _____

7. $\sqrt{18} =$ _____

4. Write $1.\overline{2}$ as a mixed number.

   _____

8. $19 - (-9) =$ _____

Directions: Solve each problem.

1. Find the distance between the two points on the graph.

$c =$ _____

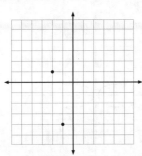

2. What is the missing side length?

$c =$ _____

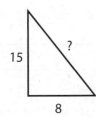

15

?

8

3. Is $\frac{19}{4}$ rational or irrational?

_____

4. Use >, <, or = to compare the numbers.

0.87 _____ $\sqrt{0.92}$

5. $\dfrac{5a^9 b^{11}}{15a^7 b^5} =$ _____

6. $x^2 = 64$

$x =$ _____

7. Plot the approximate value of $2\sqrt{10}$ on the number line.

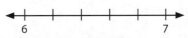

6   7

8. Does the relationship on the graph represent a proportional relationship?

_____

Cumulative Review

Name: _____ Date: _____

Directions: Solve each problem.

1. Write 5.2×10^{-2} in standard form.

_____

5. Does the relationship shown on the graph represent a function?

_____

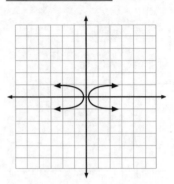

2. Write 27 as a ratio.

_____

6. Plot the approximate value of $4\sqrt{18}$ on the number line.

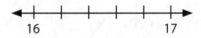

3. Which two integers is $\sqrt{89}$ between?

_____ and _____

7. What is the measure of angle *x*?

_____

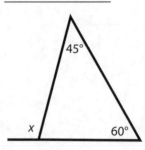

4. The trend line drawn on the graph is not accurate. Draw a more accurate trend line.

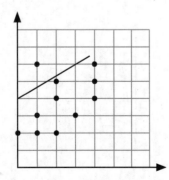

8. What is the sum of the angles of a triangle?

_____

Name: _____ **Date:** _____

Directions: Solve each problem.

1. Write 0.27 as a fraction.

   _____

2. $x^3 = 27$

   $x =$ _____

3. $4(x + 4) = 36$

   $x =$ _____

4. A cube has a volume of 36 cubic units. What is the length of each side?

   _____

5. Brady chooses a marble 210 times from a bag with 2 red marbles and 4 black marbles. How many times can he expect to choose a red marble?

   _____

6. $2[4(3 - 1) - 42] - 33 + 17 =$ _____

7. Solve the inequality, and graph the solution on the number line.

   $5x - 7 > 18$

   $x =$ _____

8. $(x^3)^4 =$ _____

Name: _____ **Date:** _____

Directions: Solve each problem.

1. Write 4.2×10^{-2} in standard form.

   _____

2. $\sqrt[3]{8} =$ _____

3. Solve the system of equations by graphing.

   $\frac{1}{3}x + y = 1$

   $y = \frac{5}{3}x - 5$

   Solution: _____

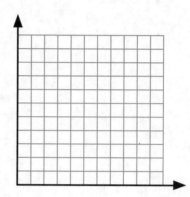

4. $(5.2 \times 10^3)(2.1 \times 10^3) =$ _____

5. The height of Mount Everest is 8,850 meters. What is the height of Mount Everest in scientific notation?

   _____

6. The height of Mount Vesuvius is 1.281×10^3 meters. Using the information from question 5, how much taller is Mount Everest than Mount Vesuvius?

   _____

7. Which number is larger, 10.3 or $\sqrt{99}$?

   _____

8. Plot the approximate location of each number on the number line.

   $\sqrt{11}$, $\sqrt{6}$, $\sqrt{8}$

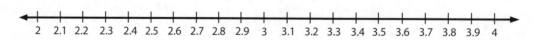

Directions: Solve each problem.

1. James is choosing a card from a standard deck. What is the probability that he will choose a card that is a heart?

_____

2. $3[5(6 - 1) - 12] - 33 + 17 =$ _____

3. $\sqrt{64} =$ _____

4. $x^3 = 8$

$x =$ _____

5. Plot the approximate location of each number on the number line.

$\sqrt{29}, \sqrt{37}, \sqrt{32}$

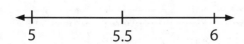

6. Which company has the lower price per card?

Company A: $y = 4.25x$ Company B

Cost ($) vs Number of Cards

7. $(3x^3)^2 =$ _____

8. Is $y = x^2$ a linear function?

_____

Cumulative Review

Name: _____ Date: _____

Directions: Solve each problem.

1. Write $0.\overline{6}$ as a fraction.

_____

2. What is the volume of the sphere?

_____

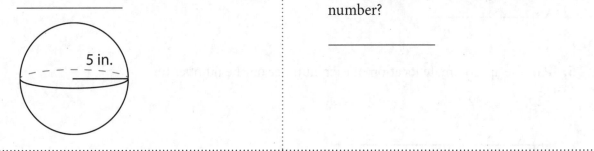

5 in.

3. Is $\sqrt{2}$ rational or irrational?

_____

4. $57.5 \times 100 + 3.3 \times 10^4 =$ _____

5. Find the mean and mean absolute deviation of the data set.

21, 29, 34, 45, 51

  a. Mean: _____

  b. MAD: _____

6. A six-sided number cube is rolled. What is the probability of rolling an odd number?

_____

7. $(7.8 \times 10^5) + (6.1 \times 10^5) =$ _____

8. Find the distance between the two plotted points.

  $c =$ _____

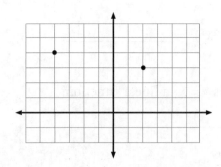

Cumulative Review

Standards Correlations

Shell Education is committed to producing educational materials that are research and standards based. To support this effort, this resource is correlated to the academic standards of all 50 states, the District of Columbia, the Department of Defense Dependent Schools, and the Canadian provinces. A correlation is also provided for key professional educational organizations.

To print a customized correlation report for your state, visit our website at **www.tcmpub.com/administrators/correlations** and follow the online directions. If you require assistance in printing correlation reports, please contact the Customer Service Department at 1-800-858-7339.

Standards Overview

The Every Student Succeeds Act (ESSA) mandates that all states adopt challenging academic standards that help students meet the goal of college and career readiness. While many states already adopted academic standards prior to ESSA, the act continues to hold states accountable for detailed and comprehensive standards. Standards are designed to focus instruction and guide adoption of curricula. They define the knowledge, skills, and content students should acquire at each level. Standards are also used to develop standardized tests to evaluate students' academic progress. State standards are used in the development of our resources, so educators can be assured they meet state academic requirements.

College and Career Readiness

Today's college and career readiness (CCR) standards offer guidelines for preparing K–12 students with the knowledge and skills that are necessary to succeed in postsecondary job training and education. CCR standards include the Common Core State Standards (CCSS) as well as other state-adopted standards such as the Texas Essential Knowledge and Skills. The standards found on pages 220–221 describe the content presented throughout this book.

English Language Development Standards

English language development standards are integrated within the practice pages to enable English learners to work toward proficiency in English while learning content—developing the skills and confidence in listening, speaking, reading, and writing.

Standards Correlations *(cont.)*

180 Days of Math for Eighth Grade offers a full page of mathematics practice activities for each day of the school year. Every unit provides questions tied to multiple math standards, giving students the opportunity for practice in a variety of mathematical concepts.

College and Career Readiness Standards

The Number System
Define rational and irrational numbers. Understand informally that every number has a decimal expansion; for rational numbers show that the decimal expansion repeats eventually, and convert a decimal expansion that repeats eventually into a rational number.
Plot, order, and compare rational numbers and rational approximations of irrational numbers, represented in various forms.

Expressions and Equations
Solve multistep mathematical and real-world problems involving the order of operations with rational numbers including exponents and radicals.
Know and apply the properties of integer exponents to generate equivalent numerical expressions.
Given an equation in the form $x^2 = p$ and $x^3 = q$, where p is a whole number and q is an integer, determine the real solutions. Evaluate square roots of small perfect squares and cube roots of small perfect cubes.
Graph proportional relationships, interpreting the unit rate as the slope of the graph. Compare two different proportional relationships represented in different ways.
Use similar triangles to explain why the slope m is the same between any two distinct points on a nonvertical line in the coordinate plane; derive the equation $y = mx$ for a line through the origin and the equation $y = mx + b$ for a line intercepting the vertical axis at b.
Give examples of linear equations in one variable and solve linear equations with rational number coefficients.
Analyze and solve pairs of simultaneous linear equations, and estimate solutions by graphing the equations.
Solve real-world and mathematical problems leading to two linear equations in two variables.

Functions
Understand and identify functions using sets of ordered pairs, tables, mappings, and graphs. Identify examples of proportional and nonproportional functions that arise from mathematical and real-world problems.
Compare properties of two functions, each represented in a different way.
Interpret the equation $y = mx + b$ as defining a linear function, whose graph is a straight line; give examples of functions that are not linear.
Construct a function to model a linear relationship between two quantities. Determine and interpret the rate of change and initial value of the function from a description of a relationship or from two (x, y) values, including reading these from a table or from a graph.

Standards Correlations *(cont.)*

Analyze a real-world written description or graphical representation of a functional relationship between two quantities and identify where the function is increasing, decreasing, or constant. Sketch a graph that exhibits the qualitative features of a function that has been described verbally.

Geometry

Verify experimentally the properties of rotations, reflections, and translations:
- Lines are taken to lines, and line segments to line segments of the same length.
- Angles are taken to angles of the same measure.
- Parallel lines are taken to parallel lines.

Understand that a two-dimensional figure is congruent to another if the second can be obtained from the first by a sequence of rotations, reflections, and translations; given two congruent figures, describe a sequence that exhibits the congruence between them.

Describe the effect of dilations, translations, rotations, and reflections on two-dimensional figures using coordinates.

Understand that a two-dimensional figure is similar to another if the second can be obtained from the first by a sequence of rotations, reflections, translations, and dilations; given two similar two-dimensional figures, describe a sequence that exhibits the similarity between them.

Use informal arguments to establish facts about the angle sum and exterior angles of triangles, about the angles created when parallel lines are cut by a transversal, and the angle-angle criterion for similarity of triangles.

Understand and apply the Pythagorean Theorem to explain a proof of the theorem and its converse, determine unknown side lengths in right triangles in real-world and mathematical problems in two and three dimensions, and find the distance between two points in a coordinate system.

Know the formulas for the volumes of cones, cylinders, and spheres and use them to solve real-world and mathematical problems.

Statistics and Probability

Construct and interpret scatter plots for bivariate measurement data to investigate patterns of association between two quantities. Describe patterns such as clustering, outliers, positive or negative association, linear association, and nonlinear association.

Know that straight lines are widely used to model relationships between two quantitative variables. For scatter plots that suggest a linear association, informally fit a straight line, and informally assess the model fit by judging the closeness of the data points to the line.

Use the equation of a linear model to solve problems in the context of bivariate measurement data, interpreting the slope and intercept.

Understand that patterns of association can also be seen in bivariate categorical data by displaying frequencies and relative frequencies in a two-way table. Construct and interpret a two-way table summarizing data on two categorical variables collected from the same subjects. Use relative frequencies calculated for rows or columns to describe possible association between the two variables.

Determine the mean absolute deviation and use this quantity as a measure of the average distance data are from the mean using a data set of no more than 10 data points.

Simulate generating random samples of the same size from a population with known characteristics to develop the notion of a random sample being representative of the population from which it was selected.

References Cited

Cathcart, W. George, Yvonne M. Pothier, James H. Vance, and Nadine S. Bezuk. 2014. *Learning Mathematics in Elementary and Middle Schools: A Learning-Centered Approach*, 6th ed. Upper Saddle River: Prentice-Hall.

Durkin, Kelley, Bethany Rittle-Johnson, and Jon R. Star. 2017. "Using Comparison of Multiple Strategies in the Mathematics Classroom: Lessons Learned and Next Steps." *ZDM: The International Journal on Mathematics Education* 49, no. 4.

Ireland, Jo and Melissa Mouthaan. 2020. "Perspectives on Curriculum Design: Comparing the Spiral and the Network Models." *Research Matters: A Cambridge Assessment Publication,* 30: 7–12.

Marchitello, Max and Megan Wilhelm. 2014. "The Cognitive Science Behind the Common Core." Center for American Progress.

McNeil, Nicole, and Linda Jarvin. 2007. "When Theories Don't Add Up: Disentangling the Manipulatives Debate." *Theory into Practice* 46, no. 4: 309–316.

Answer Key

Grade 7 Review

Day 1 (page 10)
1. circle
2. 4^5 or 1,024
3. 5
4. 56 days
5. 72
6. −4
7. $1,200
8. 0.4
9. $8\frac{17}{35}$
10. 105

Day 2 (page 11)
1. no
2. $2\frac{5}{12}$
3. $-1\frac{1}{3} + 2\frac{1}{3}$
4. $0.\overline{6}$
5. 5
6. $2x + 11$
7. 9
8.
9. 3^6 or 729
10. 20

Day 3 (page 12)
1. $6\frac{11}{40}$
2. $5(a + 5)$

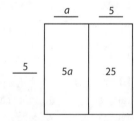

3. 180 pages
4. 75
5. $5\frac{3}{5}$ batches
6. $\frac{1}{4} - (-\frac{3}{4}) = 1$ or $0.25 - (-0.75) = 1$
7. $14.50 per hour
8. 20
9. $248.50
10. 15,840 minutes

Day 4 (page 13)
1. 0
2.
3. 20π yd.
4. supplementary
5. 19.5 in.^{2}
6. $3x + 12$
7. −8
8. 4^6 or 4,096
9. $54
10. 64 units

Day 5 (page 14)
1. 30°
2. 10
3. 5
4. 26
5. $x + 65° = 90°$; $x = 25°$
6. $14x + 21y + 56$
7.
a. 6
b. 4 hours
8. $4\frac{2}{3}$

Day 6 (page 15)
1. complementary
2. 110 in.^{2}
3. 22
4. $x + 65° = 180°$; $x = 115°$
5. 270 goldfish
6. 2 pies
7. no
8. 11 units
9. 20 books
10. 5 books

Day 7 (page 16)
1. 254.34 m^2
2. $45° + x + 40° = 180°$; $x = 95°$
3. $1,800
4. 129
5. 0.5
6. $y = 35x$
7. 14
8.

Fraction	Decimal	Percent
$\frac{3}{4}$	0.75	75%
$\frac{8}{25}$	0.32	32%
$\frac{3}{20}$	0.15	15%

9. 4 people
10. 10

Day 8 (page 17)
1. 40 yd.^{2}
2. $3x$
3. 540 in.^{3}
4. $105.80
5. 8π In.
6. yes
7. 12
8. $140.40
9. 49
10. −24

Day 9 (page 18)
1. no
2. 336 hours
3. 0.375
4. $16\frac{99}{100}$ or 16.99 miles
5. $x + 65° = 90°$; $x = 25°$
6. 56 miles
7. 10 minutes
8. $7\frac{1}{8}$
9. $6m + 5n - 6$
10. no

Day 10 (page 19)
1. 34.54 mm
2. $10x$
3. 36
4. 8
5. 5π
6. $360
7. $9\frac{1}{10}$ or 9.1 pints
8. 6 miles
9. −18
10. no

Unit 1

Learn about Rational Numbers (page 20)
Example 1
1. 0.0833
2. 0.0833
Example 2
1. 14.4
2. 0.4
3. terminating
Example 3
4. 0.151515
Example 4
1. tenths
3. $\frac{7}{5}$
Example 5
1. $-\frac{4}{1}$
2. −4.0
Example 6
1. 3.464
2. no
3. no

Answer Key (cont.)

Day 1 (page 22)

1. 0.8
2. 0.1
3. 0.875
4. 0.75
5. 0.125
6. 0.5
7. 0.6
8. 0.7
9. 0.625
10. 0.2

Day 2 (page 23)

1. $0.\overline{6}$
2. $0.8\overline{3}$
3. $0.\overline{2}$
4. $0.1\overline{6}$
5. $0.\overline{3}$
6. $0.\overline{09}$
7. $0.\overline{5}$
8. $0.41\overline{6}$
9. $0.\overline{1}$
10. $0.\overline{36}$

Day 3 (page 24)

1. 1.8; terminating
2. 1.2; terminating
3. $1.\overline{3}$; repeating
4. 3.5; terminating
5. 1.8; terminating
6. $2.\overline{6}$; repeating
7. $1.\overline{5}$; repeating
8. $5.\overline{6}$; repeating
9. 3.2; terminating
10. 3.0; terminating

Day 4 (page 25)

1. $\frac{8}{9}$
2. $\frac{16}{99}$
3. $\frac{5}{9}$
4. $\frac{2}{9}$
5. $1\frac{26}{99}$
6. $2\frac{53}{99}$
7. $\frac{25}{99}$
8. $3\frac{95}{99}$
9. $\frac{7}{9}$
10. $5\frac{9}{11}$

Day 5 (page 26)

1. $\frac{6}{5}$
2. $\frac{3}{4}$
3. $\frac{21}{4}$
4. $-\frac{42}{5}$
5. $\frac{63}{5}$
6. $\frac{9}{1}$
7. $-\frac{7}{1}$
8. $\frac{19}{2}$
9. $\frac{102}{25}$
10. $-\frac{53}{10}$

Day 6 (page 27)

1. a. $\frac{9}{1}$
   b. 9.0
2. a. $-\frac{11}{1}$
   b. −11.0
3. a. $\frac{27}{1}$
   b. 27.0
4. a. $-\frac{18}{1}$
   b. −18.0
5. a. $\frac{100}{1}$
   b. 100.0
6. a. $-\frac{50}{1}$
   b. −50.0
7. a. $\frac{3}{1}$
   b. 3.0
8. a. $-\frac{8}{1}$
   b. −8.0
9. a. $\frac{32}{1}$
   b. 32.0
10. a. $\frac{28}{1}$
    b. 28.0

Day 7 (page 28)

1. rational
2. rational
3. irrational
4. irrational
5. rational
6. rational
7. irrational
8. irrational
9. rational
10. rational
11. rational
12. irrational

Day 8 (page 29)

1. $-\frac{30}{10}, 3\frac{1}{5}, 3.5, 3\frac{5}{6}$
2. $-\frac{80}{5}, -8.75, -8\frac{3}{6}, -8$
3. $\frac{100}{11}, \frac{41}{4}, \frac{21}{2}, 10.8$
4. $\frac{65}{5}, 13\frac{3}{8}, 13.7, 13.92$
5. $-4.3, -4\frac{1}{4}, -4.15, -\frac{20}{5}$
6. $\frac{17}{8}, 2.5, \frac{14}{5}, 2\frac{9}{10}$
7. $-12.95, -12\frac{3}{5}, -12\frac{1}{4}, -\frac{120}{10}$
8. $9\frac{1}{9}, 9.2, 9\frac{2}{5}, 9.75$
9. $7\frac{1}{3}, 7\frac{1}{2}, 7.\overline{6}, 7.83$
10. $-\frac{41}{7}, -5\frac{2}{3}, -5.14, -\frac{45}{9}$
11. $1.\overline{4}, 1\frac{5}{6}, 1\frac{7}{8}, 1.94$
12. $\frac{3}{5}, \frac{7}{8}, 0.88886, \frac{8}{9}$

Day 9 (page 30)

1. $8.2, \frac{43}{5}, 8\frac{2}{3}$
2. $3\frac{3}{5}, \frac{29}{8}, 3.9$
3. $-8.5°, -3.9°, -2.7°, 1.8°, 5°$
4. $11\frac{1}{4}, 11.5, \frac{95}{8}$
5. $10\frac{1}{4}, 10\frac{3}{5}, \frac{109}{10}$
6. $\frac{131}{10}, 13\frac{3}{8}, 13.65$
7. $\frac{351}{5}, 70\frac{3}{4}, 70.9$
8. $9\frac{1}{4}, 9.5, \frac{99}{10}$

Day 10 (page 31)

1.
2.
3.
4.
5.
6.
7.
8.

Learn about Irrational Numbers (page 32)

Example 1

1. 5, 5
2. 4.123
3.

Example 2

2. a
3. c
4. b

Day 11 (page 33)

1. rational
2. rational
3. irrational
4. irrational
5. rational
6. irrational
7. rational
8. rational
9. irrational
10. rational

Day 12 (page 34)

1. 5 and 6; closer to 6
2. 3 and 4; closer to 3
3. 8 and 9; closer to 9
4. 2 and 3; closer to 2
5. 9 and 10; closer to 9
6. 6.40
7. 10.86
8. 8.06
9. 7.68
10. 5.29

Answer Key *(cont.)*

Day 13 (page 35)

1.
number line 3 to 4, $\sqrt{15}$ marked

2. number line 9 to 10, $\sqrt{85}$ marked

3. number line 4 to 5, $\sqrt{19}$ marked

4. number line 6 to 7, $\sqrt{39}$ marked

5. number line 10 to 11, $\sqrt{101}$ marked

6. number line 8 to 9, $\sqrt{78}$ marked

7. number line 3 to 4, $\sqrt{10}$ marked

8. number line 5 to 6, $\sqrt{33}$ marked

9. number line 6 to 7, $\sqrt{47}$ marked

10. number line 7 to 8, $\sqrt{53}$ marked

Day 14 (page 36)

1. **a.** $\sqrt{42}$
   b. $\sqrt{51}$
   c. $\sqrt{47}$
2. **a.** $\sqrt{75}$
   b. $\sqrt{83}$
   c. $\sqrt{91}$
3. **a.** $\sqrt{29}$
   b. $\sqrt{40}$
   c. $\sqrt{48}$
4. **a.** $\sqrt{11}$
   b. $\sqrt{18}$
   c. $\sqrt{22}$

5. **a.** $\sqrt{57}$
   b. $\sqrt{63}$
   c. $\sqrt{68}$
6. **a.** $\sqrt{39}$
   b. $\sqrt{44}$
   c. $\sqrt{48}$
7. **a.** $\sqrt{6}$
   b. $\sqrt{8}$
   c. $\sqrt{11}$
8. **a.** $\sqrt{38}$
   b. $\sqrt{42}$
   c. $\sqrt{47}$

Day 15 (page 37)

1. <   **6.** >   **11.** <
2. <   **7.** <   **12.** <
3. >   **8.** >
4. <   **9.** <
5. <   **10.** >

Day 16 (page 38)

1. $\sqrt{83}$, 9.5, $\sqrt{101}$, $10\frac{9}{10}$
2. $\sqrt{42}$, $\sqrt{48}$, 7.5, $7\frac{7}{8}$
3. $3\frac{1}{8}$, π, $\frac{16}{5}$, $\sqrt{15}$
4. $7\frac{1}{10}$, $\sqrt{63}$, $\sqrt{65}$, 8.7
5. $5\frac{1}{3}$, 5.6, $\sqrt{35}$, $\sqrt{39}$
6. $\sqrt{65}$, $\sqrt{71}$, $\sqrt{78}$, 8.9
7. $\frac{101}{10}$, 10.4, $\sqrt{120}$, $\sqrt{122}$
8. $\sqrt{10}$, 3.4, $\sqrt{15}$, 4.2
9. 7.6, $\sqrt{62}$, 8, $\frac{43}{5}$
10. 6.3, 7.1, $\sqrt{55}$, $\sqrt{60}$
11. $\sqrt{99}$, $\sqrt{102}$, $10\frac{8}{9}$, 10.9
12. $\sqrt{7}$, $\frac{14}{5}$, 2.9, $\sqrt{11}$

Day 17 (page 39)

1. $\sqrt{8}$ **7.** 11.1
2. 3.9   **8.** $\sqrt{10}$
3. 9.2   **9.** 6.5
4. 7.8   **10.** $\frac{76}{10}$
5. $\sqrt{108}$ **11.** $9.\overline{3}$
6. π **12.** $\sqrt{20}$

Day 18 (page 40)

1. 7.83   **8.** 8.87
2. 9.42   **9.** 26.83
3. 10   **10.** 11.90
4. 10.47   **11.** 12.73
5. 8.27   **12.** 25.13
6. 11.46   **13.** 12.54
7. 12.65   **14.** 6

Day 19 (page 41)

1. 4.45
number line 4 to 5, $2+\sqrt{6}$ marked

2. 7.94
number line 7 to 8, $3\sqrt{7}$ marked

3. 10.14
number line 10 to 11, $\sqrt{51}+3$ marked

4. 3.76
number line 3 to 4, $8-\sqrt{18}$ marked

5. 9.38
number line 9 to 10, $2\sqrt{22}$ marked

6. 9.42
number line 9 to 10, 3π marked

7. 3.28
number line 3 to 4, $12-\sqrt{76}$ marked

8. 9.59
number line 9 to 10, $2\sqrt{23}$ marked

9. 6.24
number line 6 to 7, $4+\sqrt{5}$ marked

10. 8.16
number line 8 to 9, $\sqrt{10}+5$ marked

Day 20 (page 42)

1. 3, 4
2. 9, 10
3. 10, 11
4. 5, 6
5. **a.** $\sqrt{52}$
   b. $\sqrt{57}$
   c. $\sqrt{66}$
6. **a.** $\sqrt{99}$
   b. $\sqrt{105}$
   c. $\sqrt{110}$
7. number line 8 to 9, $\sqrt{65}$ marked
8. number line 9 to 10, $\sqrt{98}$ marked
9. number line 3 to 4, $\sqrt{10}$ marked
10. number line 7 to 8, $\sqrt{52}$ marked

Day 21 (page 43)

1. $\sqrt{17}$, 4.5, $\sqrt{32}$, 6.4
2. $\sqrt{110}$
3. <
4. 0.125
5. 7.3, $\frac{37}{5}$, $7\frac{8}{9}$, $\frac{40}{5}$
6. 5.25
7. repeating
8. 7, 8
9. $-\frac{3}{1}$
10. yes

Appendix

Answer Key *(cont.)*

Day 22 (page 44)

1.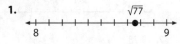
   $\sqrt{77}$ between 8 and 9

2. $\sqrt{19}$ $\sqrt{21}$ $\sqrt{24}$ between 4, 4.5, 5

3. -4.0

4. $\frac{41}{5}$ pounds, $8\frac{5}{9}$ pounds, 8.75 pounds, 8.9 pounds

5. terminating

6. $\frac{2}{9}$

7. a. $\frac{32}{5}$
   b. $-\frac{8}{1}$
   c. $\frac{23}{100}$

8. 3.14

9. $>$

10. Answers should include an example of an irrational number.

Day 23 (page 45)

1. a. $\sqrt{35}$
   b. $\sqrt{40}$
   c. 6.5

2. Answers should include an example of a whole number.

3. $\sqrt{27}$ $\sqrt{31}$ $\sqrt{39}$ between 5, 5.5, 6

4. $\frac{5}{11}$

5. 1.875

6. $\sqrt{51}$ between 7 and 8

7. $\sqrt{76}$

8. terminating

9. $6 \times \sqrt{46}$ between 40 and 41

10. $-4.67, -\frac{9}{2}, -4\frac{1}{4}, -4.2$

Day 24 (page 46)

1. Answers should include an example of an integer.

2. 1.4

3.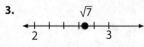
   $\sqrt{7}$ between 2 and 3

4. a. $\sqrt{17}$
   b. $4\frac{3}{8}$
   c. 4.8

5. 7.81

6. 4.2

7. $\frac{41}{5}$

8. 7

9. 6.76

10. $\frac{7}{9}$

Day 25 (page 47)

1. $\sqrt{41}$ between 6 and 7

2. $\sqrt{6}$ $\sqrt{10}$ $\sqrt{14}$ between 2, 2.5, 3, 3.5

3. 20.11

4. $\frac{26}{1}$

5. $\frac{35}{99}$

6. a. 7.01
   b. $7\frac{1}{4}$
   c. $\sqrt{59}$

7. $8.98, 9\frac{3}{8}, \sqrt{144}$

8.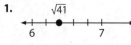
   $\sqrt{118}$ between 10 and 11

9. irrational; π cannot be expressed as a ratio of integers

10. $<$

Unit 2

Day 1 (page 49)

1. 1
2. f
3. g^7
4. k^{11}
5. y
6. 1
7. w^{12}
8. 1
9. q^{10}
10. b^2
11. 4^5
12. 6

Day 2 (page 50)

1. y^2
2. ab^2
3. 4
4. h^3
5. 7^3
6. $\frac{w^{18}}{x^6}$
7. $x^2y^2z^3$
8. 9^2
9. p^8
10. jk^7
11. 6
12. $\frac{k^{15}}{m^9}$

Day 3 (page 51)

1. m^{12}
2. $a^{20}b^{15}$
3. $4^4 = 256$
4. x^{42}
5. w^4y^6
6. h^{27}
7. $b^{16}c^8$
8. z^{63}
9. 1
10. $p^{30}q^{12}$
11. $3^4 = 81$
12. $x^{40}y^{16}$

Day 4 (page 52)

1. $\frac{1}{d^2}$
2. $\frac{1}{5^3}$
3. $\frac{1}{x^6}$
4. $\frac{1}{4^2}$
5. $\frac{1}{7^2}$
6. $\frac{1}{a^4}$
7. $\frac{n^2}{m^4}$
8. $\frac{1}{w^6}$
9. $\frac{1}{p^3}$
10. $\frac{1}{8^3}$
11. $\frac{1}{h^5}$
12. $\frac{y}{x}$

Day 5 (page 53)

1. 1
2. t
3. g^{12}
4. y^{54}
5. $4^3 = 64$
6. $\frac{m^{20}}{n^{15}}$
7. $5^4 = 625$
8. y^2
9. x^7y^5
10. k
11. $\frac{1}{p^5}$
12. f^8

Day 6 (page 55)

1. 16
2. 125
3. 1
4. 81
5. 343
6. 27
7. 64
8. 25
9. 121
10. 216
11. 64
12. 4
13. 49
14. 1,000

Day 7 (page 56)

1. 12
2. a
3. xy
4. 8
5. 11
6. m
7. 3
8. 9
9. g
10. ab
11. 10
12. $\frac{1}{2}$

Day 8 (page 57)

1. 5
2. x
3. 4
4. 3
5. 6
6. a
7. 8
8. 1
9. 9
10. gh
11. 2
12. 10

Answer Key *(cont.)*

Day 9 (page 58)

1. 7	**5.** 1	**9.** 13
2. 4	**6.** 6	**10.** 3
3. 10	**7.** 5	**11.** 15
4. 11	**8.** 2	**12.** 7

Day 10 (page 59)

1. 343	**6.** 10	**11.** 6
2. 400	**7.** w	**12.** 4
3. 256	**8.** 10	**13.** 6
4. 8	**9.** 1	**14.** 7
5. $\frac{1}{4}$	**10.** 1	

Learn about Multistep Problem Solving (page 60)

Example 1
12
Example 2
2. $x = 9$

Day 11 (page 61)

1. 27	**6.** 45	**11.** 504
2. 64	**7.** 327	**12.** 24
3. 125	**8.** 264	**13.** 8
4. 1	**9.** 86	**14.** 672
5. 16	**10.** 117	

Day 12 (page 62)

1. 9	**5.** 5	**9.** 2
2. 4	**6.** 13	**10.** 9
3. 5	**7.** 3	**11.** 8
4. 2	**8.** 13	**12.** 12

Day 13 (page 63)

1. $4\frac{1}{9}$	**5.** 3	**9.** −38
2. 13	**6.** $125\frac{1}{4}$	**10.** 11
3. $84\frac{1}{8}$	**7.** −8	**11.** −1
4. 51	**8.** −22	**12.** 1

Day 14 (page 64)

1. 8 feet	**6.** 12 centimeters
2. 11 feet	**7.** 9 centimeters
3. 5 centimeters	**8.** 7 meters
4. 10 yards	**9.** 7 centimeters
5. 8 inches	**10.** 12 meters

Day 15 (page 65)

1. 44	**7.** 14
2. 52	**8.** −96
3. 16	**9.** −16
4. 15	**10.** −115
5. 4	**11.** 10 inches
6. 2	**12.** 13 feet

Learn about Scientific Notation (page 66)

Example 1
1. 6
Example 2
1. 4
Example 4
2. 295
Example 5
1. 3.15
2. 5
Example 6
1. 2
2. 1

Day 16 (page 68)

1. 5.4×10^8	**8.** 5.1×10^{-5}
2. 1.8×10^3	**9.** 6.8×10^{-3}
3. 8.9×10^{-7}	**10.** 2.3×10^{12}
4. 6.7×10^9	**11.** 6.5×10^7
5. 3.2×10^{-9}	**12.** 3.5×10^{-8}
6. 8.7×10^4	**13.** 5.3×10^{-2}
7. 4.5×10^{-4}	**14.** 6.03×10^6

Day 17 (page 69)

1. 120,000
2. 0.00036
3. 8,700
4. 0.000000066
5. 0.000058
6. 0.0083
7. 74,000,000
8. 0.018
9. 39,000
10. 2,400
11. 0.0000000083
12. 6,200,000
13. 0.91
14. 470,000,000

Day 18 (page 70)

1. 6.5×10^4	**8.** 1.48×10^{-3}
2. 1.4×10^{-5}	**9.** 5.69×10^4
3. 4.03×10^3	**10.** 1.1×10^6
4. 8.88×10^7	**11.** 2.38×10^{10}
5. 6.94×10^{-6}	**12.** 3.775×10^{-3}
6. 7.39×10^9	
7. 5×10^{-6}	

Day 19 (page 71)

1. 9.43×10^{10}	**7.** 2.5×10^3
2. 6.46×10^{-11}	**8.** 4×10^{-1}
3. 3.485×10^9	**9.** 4×10^{12}
4. 6.11×10^{-11}	**10.** 1.2×10^1
5. 3.599×10^7	**11.** 1.4×10^{16}
6. 1.533×10^{-1}	**12.** 6.5×10^{-10}

Day 20 (page 72)

1. 9.03×10^7 square yards
2. 5×10^{11} tons of strawberries
3. 3.751×10^8 miles
4. 2.508×10^{25} molecules
5. 4×10^7 meters per second
6. 0.0024 inches
7. 4×10^{-3} inches
8. 2.892×10^8 ounces
9. 1.3×10^4 kilograms
10. 3.7×10^4 kilograms

Learn about Proportional Relationships and Slope (page 73)

Example 1
2. $\frac{4}{1}$, goes up by 4
Example 2
1. (1,1), (5,5)
3. $\frac{1}{1}$

Day 21 (page 74)

1. a.

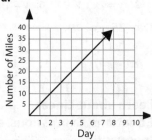

b. 5

2. a.

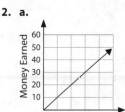

b. 10

Answer Key (cont.)

3. a.

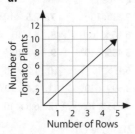

b. 2

4. a.

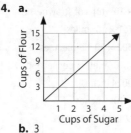

b. 3

Day 22 (page 75)

1. Marty's Market
2. Store A
3. Streaming Service B
4. Babysitter B

Day 23 (page 76)

1. 1
2. $\frac{3}{2}$
3. 3
4. 1
5. $\frac{1}{2}$
6. 3

Day 24 (page 77)

1. $y = \frac{2}{3}x + 4$
2. $y = \frac{1}{2}x$
3. $y = \frac{1}{4}x + 1$
4. $y = \frac{5}{2}x$
5. $y = x + 4$
6. $y = \frac{4}{3}x$

Day 25 (page 78)

1. 1, 1
2. −1, −1
3. $\frac{3}{2}, \frac{3}{2}$
4. 1, 1
5. $\frac{5}{2}, \frac{5}{2}$
6. −1, −1

Learn about Linear Equations, Expressions, and Inequalities (page 79)

Example 3
4. 1
5. $\frac{1}{3}$

Example 4
4. $16

Day 26 (page 81)

1. 11
2. 18
3. −3
4. 1
5. 13
6. 9
7. 19
8. −34
9. 7
10. 3
11. 11
12. −9
13. −1
14. −11

Day 27 (page 82)

1. **a.** 24 = 24
   b. infinite solutions
2. **a.** −10 = 12
   b. no solution
3. **a.** x = 6
   b. one solution
4. **a.** −9 = −14
   b. no solution
5. **a.** $x = \frac{7}{5}$
   b. one solution
6. **a.** −8 = −28
   b. no solution
7. **a.** x = 4
   b. one solution
8. **a.** 12 = 12
   b. infinite solutions
9. **a.** −15 = −15
   b. infinite solutions
10. **a.** x = 6
    b. one solution

Day 28 (page 83)

1. −5
2. 4
3. $\frac{1}{3}$
4. −1
5. $-\frac{1}{8}$
6. 0
7. 2
8. 2
9. −4
10. 9

Day 29 (page 84)

1. **a.** x < 12
   b.

2. **a.** x ≥ 4
   b.
3. **a.** x > 6
   b.
4. **a.** x ≤ 5
   b.
5. **a.** x > 4
   b.

6. **a.** x < 6
   b.

7. **a.** x ≥ 3
   b.

8. **a.** x ≥ 3
   b.

Day 30 (page 85)

1. **a.** 3x + 30 = 120
   b. x = 30; Myra needs to paint 30 feet each day.
2. **a.** 4x + 12 ≤ 48
   b. x ≤ 9; Each package of posterboard can cost at most $9.
3. **a.** 4(x + 2) = 56
   b. x = 12; Each sandwich cost $12.
4. **a.** 3x + 26 ≤ 182
   b. x ≤ 52; Each video game is at most $52.
5. **a.** 5x + 40 = 320
   b. x = 56; Each sweater was $56.
6. **a.** 7x + 7 = 35
   b. x = 4; Each bottle of sports drink cost $4.
7. **a.** 3(x + 6) ≤ 60
   b. x ≤ 14; Each entrée is at most $14.
8. **a.** 3x + 21 = 48
   b. x = 9; Sean paid $9 for each package of cookies.

Learn about Simultaneous Equations (page 86)

Solve Graphically
2. yes
2. (1,4)

Day 31 (page 88)

1. no
2. yes
3. yes
4. no
5. yes
6. no
7. yes
8. no

Answer Key *(cont.)*

Day 32 (page 89)

1. a.
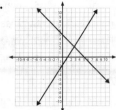

b. (2.4, 1.6)

2. a.
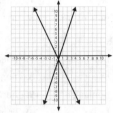

b. (0, –1)

3. a.
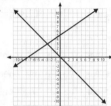

b. (–3, 3)

4. a.
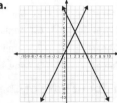

b. (2, 5)

Day 33 (page 90)

1. a.
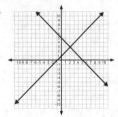

b. one solution: (2, 3)

2. a.
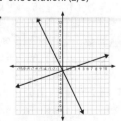

b. one solution: (0, –1)

3. a.
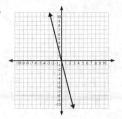

b. infinite solutions

4. a.
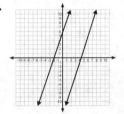

b. no solution

Day 34 (page 91)

1. (8, –4)   **5.** (3, 2)
2. (4, 4)   **6.** (7, –1)
3. (6, 6)   **7.** (–4, 34)
4. (24, –2)   **8.** (8, 24)

Day 35 (page 92)

1. a.
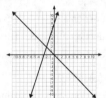

b. (–2, 2)

2. a.
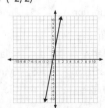

b. infinite solutions
3. no
4. no
5. no solution
6. infinite solutions

Day 36 (page 93)

1. Gym B
2. 1,728
3. 6.8×10^2
4. $\frac{31}{1}$
5. 3.61
6. 12
7. $\frac{4}{9}$
8.
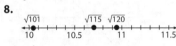
9. a. 10 and 11
   b. 11
   c. 10.77
10. 17.2

Day 37 (page 94)

1. (–2, 2)   **4.** no
2. a. $\sqrt{75}$ **5.** 3.68×10^{10}
   b. $9\frac{1}{5}$ **6.** $4.\overline{6}$
   c. $\sqrt{88}$ **7.** $4\frac{1}{4}$
3. $\frac{14}{5}$ or $2\frac{4}{5}$
8. a. $x < 8$
   b.
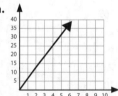

Day 38 (page 95)

1. 4×10^2
2. yes
3. a.

b. yes
   c. 6.5
4. 7
5. 0
6. 23.75
7. 3.3×10^4
8. yes
9. 15
10. 73

Answer Key *(cont.)*

Day 39 (page 96)

1. **a.** 3.25
   b. $3\frac{5}{9}$
   c. $\sqrt{15}$
2. 4.48×10^8
3. (1, 2)

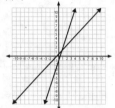

4. 2.8
5. 7.6×10^7
6. 12
7. n
8.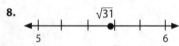
9. 43
10. 0.57

Day 40 (page 97)

1. (−9, 52)
2. Pizza Palace
3.

5 + √33
9.6   10   11

4. 169
5. **a.** 1
   b. 1
6. 2.86×10^3
7. 10
8. 8

Unit 3

Learn about Functions (page 98)

Example 1
1. yes
Example 2
1. no
Example 3
2. yes
Example 4
2, 1, 4, 7, 10
Example 5
1. 2, 2, 2

Day 1 (page 100)

1. yes
2. yes
3. yes
4. no; Each input value has two output values.
5. yes
6. yes

Day 2 (page 101)

1. 8, 20, 28, 40
2. −8, −10, −12, −14
3. 3, −5, −9, −11
4. 6, −14, 16, −20
5. −2, −1, 1, 2
6. 4, 2, −2, −4
7. nonproportional
8. nonproportional
9. proportional
10. proportional
11. proportional
12. nonproportional

Day 3 (page 102)

1. Function A
2. Function A
3. Function B
4. Function A
5. Function B
6. Function A

Day 4 (page 103)

1. Function B
2. Function B
3. Function A
4. Function A
5. Function A
6. Function A

Day 5 (page 104)

1. Plan A
2. Car B
3. Willie's Wheels
4. Kaia
5. Gym A
6. Gio

Learn about Linear and Nonlinear Functions (page 105)

Example 1
1. $\frac{4}{1}$ add 4
2. 4
3. $y = 4$
Example 2
1. no
2. no
Example 3
1. no
   a. yes
   b. nonlinear

Day 6 (page 106)

1. linear
2. nonlinear
3. linear
4. linear
5. nonlinear
6. linear
7. linear
8. linear

Day 7 (page 107)

1. linear
2. nonlinear
3. linear
4. nonlinear
5. linear
6. nonlinear
7. linear
8. nonlinear

Day 8 (page 108)

1. nonlinear
2. linear
3. nonlinear
4. linear
5. nonlinear
6. linear
7. linear
8. nonlinear
9. nonlinear
10. linear
11. linear
12. linear

Day 9 (page 109)

1. linear
2. linear
3. linear
4. linear
5. nonlinear
6. linear
7. nonlinear
8. linear

Day 10 (page 110)

1. linear
2. linear
3. linear
4. linear
5. linear
6. nonlinear
7. nonlinear
8. linear

Learn about Rate of Change
(page 111)

Example 1
1. $\frac{1}{1}$
2. −2
3. $y = x - 2$
Example 2
1. −2
2. 2
3. $y = -2x + 2$

Day 11 (page 112)

1. $y = 2x + 1$
2. $y = 5x - 4$
3. $y = 5x$
4. $y = \frac{1}{5}x$ or $y = \frac{x}{5}$ or $y = 0.2x$
5. $y = 2x - 10$
6. $y = x + 2$
7. $y = \frac{1}{2}x$ or $y = \frac{x}{2}$ or $y = 0.5x$
8. $y = x - 7$
9. $y = 5x$
10. $y = 3x + 2$

Answer Key *(cont.)*

Day 12 (page 113)
1. **a.** 10
   b. 10
2. **a.** 2
   b. 0
3. **a.** $\frac{5}{2}$ or 2.5
   b. 15
4. **a.** $\frac{1}{5}$ or 0.2
   b. 0
5. **a.** −10
   b. 60
6. **a.** 2
   b. 8

Day 13 (page 114)
1. **a.** $20
   b. $40
   c. $y = 40x + 20$
2. **a.** $40
   b. $15
   c. $y = 15x + 40$
3. **a.** $8
   b. $9
   c. $y = 9x + 8$
4. **a.** $60
   b. $80
   c. $y = 80x + 60$
5. **a.** $75
   b. $4
   c. $y = 4x + 75$
6. **a.** $40
   b. $25
   c. $y = 25x + 40$

Day 14 (page 115)
1. **a.** $50
   b. $50
   c. $y = 50x + 50$
2. **a.** $15
   b. $2
   c. $y = 2x + 15$
3. **a.** $40
   b. $20
   c. $y = 20x + 40$
4. **a.** $140
   b. $20
   c. $y = -20x + 140$ or $y = 140 - 20x$

Day 15 (page 116)
1. $y = -20x + 140$ or $y = 140 - 20x$
2. $y = 9x + 35$
3. $y = 11x + 3.50$
4. $y = 4x$
5. $y = 8x + 12$
6. $y = 2x + 3$
7. $y = 5x + 20$
8. $y = 30x + 60$

Learn about Graphing Funtional Relationships
(page 117)
Example 1
2. yes
3. increase

Day 16 (page 118)
1. c   3. a   5. b
2. a   4. d   6. c

Day 17 (page 119)
1. linear   4. nonlinear

2. nonlinear   5. linear

3. linear   6. nonlinear

Day 18 (page 120)
1. Answers should include a scenario that matches the graph.
2. Answers should include a scenario that matches the graph.
3. Answers should include a scenario that matches the graph.
4. Answers should include a scenario that matches the graph.
5. Answers should include a scenario that matches the graph.
6. Answers should include a scenario that matches the graph.

Day 19 (page 121)
1. linear   6. nonlinear
2. nonlinear   7. linear
3. nonlinear   8. linear
4. linear   9. nonlinear
5. linear   10. linear

Day 20 (page 122)
1. a
2.

3. linear
4. Answers should include a story that matches the graph.
5. a
6. nonlinear

Day 21 (page 123)
1. m
2. −9
3. **a.** $x < 10$
   b.

   ```
   -12-11-10-9-8-7-6-5-4-3-2-1 0 1 2 3 4 5 6 7 8 9 10 11 12
   ```

4. 0.625
5.

   ```
        √67          √78          √89
   +--+--+--+--+--+--+--+--+--+--+--+
   8          8.5          9        9.5
   ```

6. 9
7. yes
8. yes
9. 8.7×10^7
10. $\frac{14}{3}$

Day 22 (page 124)
1. no   6. 10
2. x^{20} 7. yes
3. $-3.9, -3\frac{1}{8},$ 8. 8
   $-\frac{23}{8}, -\sqrt{6}$ 9. no
4. 4.42×10^7 10. 180
5. 3, 7, 11, 15, 19

Answer Key *(cont.)*

Day 23 (page 125)

1. 2.2×10^6
2. yes
3. 729
4. a.

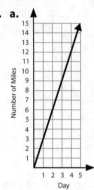

   b. 3
5. 8.84×10^9
6. no
7. x^2y^4
8. 51
9. yz
10. 0.0000085

Day 24 (page 126)

1. 3×10^1
2. a. −3
   b. −3
3. no
4. $y = 2x$
5. no solution
6. a. $x \le -8$
   b.

   -10 -9 -8 -7 -6 -5 -4 -3 -2 -1 0 1 2 3 4 5 6 7 8 9 10

7. $\frac{8}{9}$
8. nonlinear
9. 5,700,000
10. 8

Day 25 (page 127)

1. yes
2. 7.78×10^4
3. 25
4. a. $30
   b. $1.50
   c. $c = 1.5n + 30$
5. Answers should include a story that matches the graph.
6. 12
7. 2 and 3
8. $y = -\frac{5}{2}x - 5$ or $y = -2.5x - 5$

Unit 4

Learn about Transformations
(page 128)

Example 2

1. 3
2. 2
3. congruent
4. yes

Day 1 (page 130)

1. c
2. b
3. a
4. b
5. d
6. b

Day 2 (page 131)

1. 180°
   a. *WZ*
   b. *W'Z'*
   c. 1 unit
   d. yes
2. 90°
   a. *AB*
   b. *A'B'*
   c. 3 units
   d. yes
3. 270°
   a. *A'B'*
   b. *B'C'*
   c. 2 units
   d. yes

Day 3 (page 132)

1.

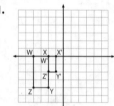

2.

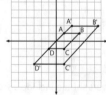

3.

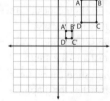

4.

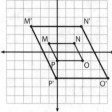

5.

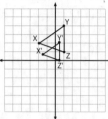

6.

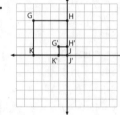

Day 4 (page 133)

1.

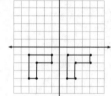

2.

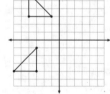

3.

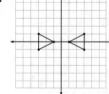

4.

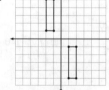

Answer Key *(cont.)*

5.

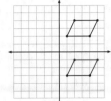

6.

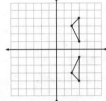

Day 5 (page 134)

1. 3
2. 4
3. $1\frac{1}{2}$
4. $\frac{1}{2}$
5. 2
6. $1\frac{1}{2}$

Day 6 (page 135)

1. translation and reflection
2. translation and reflection
3. translation and translation
4. translation and reflection OR rotation and translation
5. translation and reflection OR rotation and translation
6. rotation and reflection OR rotation and translation

Day 7 (page 136)

1. a. no
   b. Sample answer: Side lengths are not the same.
2. a. yes
   b. reflection over x-axis and reflection over y-axis
3. a. no
   b. Sample answer: Side lengths are not the same.
4. a. yes
   b. rotation and translation

Day 8 (page 137)

1. a. no
   b. yes
   c. 8 square units
   d. 2 square units
2. a. yes
   b. translation over y-axis
   c. angle W'
   d. side Z'Y'

3. a. no
   b. yes
   c. 2 units
   d. 4 units
4. a. yes
   b. rotation
   c. angle B'
   d. side B'C'

Day 9 (page 138)

1. a. $\frac{1}{2}$
   b. no
   c. yes
   d. $\frac{2}{4} = \frac{1}{2}$
   e. $\frac{1}{2}$
   f. yes
2. a. 2
   b. no
   c. yes
   d. $\frac{3}{3} = 1$
   e. $\frac{6}{6} = 1$
   f. yes
3. a. $1\frac{1}{2}$
   b. no
   c. yes
   d. $\frac{4}{1} = 4$
   e. $\frac{6}{1.5} = 4$
   f. yes

Day 10 (page 139)

1. a. dilation
   b. no
   c. yes; $\frac{1}{2}$
2. a. dilation
   b. no
   c. yes; $\frac{1}{2}$
3. a. reflection
   b. A'C'
4. a. translation
   b. yes

Learn about Angle Relationships (page 140)

Example 1

2. 153 degrees
3. 153 degrees
4. 27 degrees

Day 11 (page 142)

1. 150°
2. 115°
3. 150°
4. 120°
5. 155°
6. 103°
7. 150°
8. 85°

Day 12 (page 143)

1. 130°
2. 50°
3. 130°
4. 50°
5. 50°
6. 130°
7. 130°
8. 110°
9. 70°
10. 110°
11. 70°
12. 70°
13. 110°
14. 70°

Day 13 (page 144)

1. yes
2. no
3. yes
4. no
5. yes
6. yes

Day 14 (page 145)

1. 720°
2. 540°
3. 1,080°
5. 900°

4. 1,440°
6. 1,800°

Day 15 (page 146)

1. Sample answer: 1 and 2, and 3 and 4
2. Sample answer: 1 and 7, and 3 and 5
3. Sample answer: 1 and 3, and 2 and 4
4. h
5. 131°
6. 49°
7. 115°
8. 125°
9. 50°
10. 122°

Learn about Pythagorean Theorem (page 147)

Example 3

1. leg

Day 16 (page 149)

1. 25
2. $\sqrt{145} \approx 12.04$
3. 20
4. $\sqrt{424} \approx 20.59$
5. $\sqrt{2,664} \approx 51.61$
6. 37
7. $\sqrt{65} \approx 8.06$
8. $\sqrt{277} \approx 16.64$

Day 17 (page 150)

1. $\sqrt{525} \approx 22.91$
2. $\sqrt{612} \approx 24.74$
3. 11
4. $\sqrt{55} \approx 7.42$
5. $\sqrt{351} \approx 18.73$
6. $\sqrt{189} \approx 13.75$
7. $\sqrt{1,200} \approx 34.64$
8. $\sqrt{76} \approx 8.72$

Day 18 (page 151)

1. yes
2. no
3. yes
4. no
5. no
6. yes
7. yes
8. yes

Answer Key (cont.)

Day 19 (page 152)
1. $\sqrt{20} \approx 4.47$
2. $\sqrt{10} \approx 3.16$
3. $\sqrt{13} \approx 3.61$
4. $\sqrt{8} \approx 2.83$
5. $\sqrt{17} \approx 4.12$
6. $\sqrt{18} \approx 4.24$
7. $\sqrt{13} \approx 3.61$
8. $\sqrt{20} \approx 4.47$

Day 20 (page 153)
1. $\sqrt{1,696} \approx 41.18$
2. $\sqrt{1,200} \approx 34.64$
3. $\sqrt{140} \approx 11.83$
4. $\sqrt{261} \approx 16.16$
5. $\sqrt{698} \approx 26.42$
6. 24
7. $\sqrt{13} \approx 3.61$
8. $\sqrt{17} \approx 4.12$

Day 21 (page 155)
1. 1,582.56 cm³
2. 116.9336 cm³
3. 1,413 in.³
4. 235.5 mm³
5. 5,086.8 mm³
6. 443.1168 in.³

Day 22 (page 156)
1. 376.8 in.³
2. 461.58 mm³
3. 1,205.76 cm³
4. $366\frac{1}{3}$ ft.³
5. 3,140 mm³
6. 3,315.84 ft.³

Day 23 (page 157)
1. $523\frac{1}{3}$ in.³
2. 3,052.08 in.³
3. $5,572\frac{34}{75}$ in.³
4. 904.32 ft.³
5. 7.23456 cm³
6. 1498.454053 mm³

Day 24 (page 158)
1. approx. 1.282 ft.³
2. $4,186\frac{2}{3}$ in.³
3. approx. 35.239 in.³
4. 6.28 in.³
5. $\frac{157}{300}$ ft.³ or approx. 0.523 ft.³
6. 50.24 in.³
7. approx. 89.752 in.³
8. 1,004.8 cm³

Day 25 (page 159)
1. 692.37 in.³
2. approx. 62.146 cm³
3. approx. 434.672 in.³
4. 5.29875 ft.³
5. approx. 133.973 in.³
6. 384,650 cm³
7. 76,930 cm³
8. approx. 4,641.832 cm³

Day 26 (page 160)
1. Sample answer: 1 and 4
2. Sample answer: 1 and 2
3. Sample answer: 1 and 5
4. 135°
5. $\frac{5}{9}$
6.
7. reflection and translation
8. $\frac{1}{3}x^2$
9. $-3\frac{4}{5}, -3.2, -\frac{20}{8}, 3\frac{1}{5}$
10. 4.125

Day 27 (page 161)
1. a. $\frac{166}{5}$
   b. 33.2
2.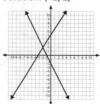
3.
4. yes
5. 0
6. nonlinear
7. yes
8. 6.7×10^3

Day 28 (page 162)
1. $\sqrt{20} \approx 4.47$
2. Solution: (−2, 2)

3. a. $x \le 5$
   b.
4. a. 1
   b. 1
5. 9.9×10^6
6. $11 - \sqrt{99}$

7. xy

Day 29 (page 163)
1.
2. a. $80
   b. $60
   c. $y = 60x + 80$
3. a. $y = 3x + 2$
   b. infinite solutions
4. no
5. $y = \frac{2}{3}x$
6. no
7. $\sqrt{58}$ $\sqrt{65}$ $\sqrt{71}$
   7.5   8   8.5   9
8. 55°

Day 30 (page 164)
1. 2
2. $\sqrt{17} \approx 4.12$
3. 12
4. no
5. $\frac{1}{5}$
6. Company B
7. $\frac{17}{99}$
8. 13

Unit 5

Learn about Scatterplots and Bivariate Data (page 165)

Example 1
1. increasing

Example 2
1. no

Day 1 (page 166)
1.
2.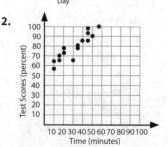

Answer Key *(cont.)*

3.

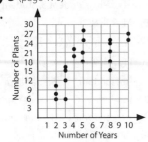

Number of Hot Dogs Sold vs Stand Number

4.

Number of Apples Picked vs Day

Day 2 (page 167)

1. positive association
2. no association
3. no association
4. negative association
5. negative association
6. positive association

Day 3 (page 168)

1. nonlinear association
2. linear association
3. nonlinear association
4. nonlinear association
5. linear association
6. linear association

Day 4 (page 169)

1. **a.** positive
   b. outlier
   c. yes
2. **a.** none
   b. cluster
   c. no
3. **a.** negative
   b. no
   c. yes
4. **a.** positive
   b. weak
   c. no

Day 5 (page 170)

1.

Number of Plants vs Number of Years

   a. positive association
   b. linear association
   c. no

---

2. **a.** no association
   b. nonlinear association
   c. no
3. **a.** negative association
   b. linear association
   c. no
4. **a.** no association
   b. nonlinear association
   c. yes

Learn about Trend Lines
(page 171)

Example 1

2. 0.025
3. $y = 0.025x$

Day 6 (page 172)

1. b.	**3.** a.	**5.** a.
2. b.	**4.** a.	**6.** a.

Day 7 (page 173)

1. 4.

2. 5.

3. 6.

Day 8 (page 174)

1. Sample answer: $y = \frac{5}{12}x$
2. Sample answer: $y = \frac{3}{5}x + 25$
3. Sample answer: $y = -\frac{20}{3}x + 30$
4. Sample answer: $y = 2x + 2$
5. Sample answer: $y = 2x$
6. Sample answer: $y = -x + 25$

Day 9 (page 175)

1. a	**3.** a	**5.** b
2. b	**4.** a	**6.** a

Day 10 (page 176)

1. Answers should be based on the trend line drawn.
2. Answers should be based on the trend line drawn.
3. Answers should be based on the trend line drawn.
4. Answers should be based on the trend line drawn.
5. a
6. b

Day 11 (page 177)

1. **a.** positive association
   b. 200
   c. Everett's intial amount of savings is $200.
   d. 100
   e. Everett saves $100 each month.
   f. $1,400
2. **a.** positive association
   b. 0
   c. Jasmine spends $0 after 0 minutes at the mall.
   d. 1.25
   e. Jasmine spends $1.25 per minute at the mall.
   f. $500
3. **a.** negative association
   b. 100
   c. A student that spends 0 hours playing sports has a grade of 100.
   d. −5
   e. A student's grade decreases by 5 percentage points for each additional hour playing sports.
   f. 75

Day 12 (page 178)

1. **a.** 8
   b. The cost of each T-shirt is $8.
   c. 25
   d. There is an initial cost of $25.
   e. $185

Answer Key *(cont.)*

2. **a.** withdrawing; The slope is negative.

   b. −20

   c. Darrah's bank account decreases by $20 each week.

   d. 200

   e. Darrah's bank account initially has $200.

3. **a.** 0.75

   b. Strawberries weigh 0.75 pounds per pint.

   c. 0

   d. 0 pints of strawberries weigh 0 pounds.

   e. 7.5 pounds

4. **a.** −100

   b. The number of pencils decreases by 100 per week.

   c. 500

   d. Mrs. Jamison initially has 500 pencils.

   e. 0 pencils

Day 13 (page 179)

1. **a.** Trend lines should represent the relationship between time and distance walked.

   b. Equations should represent the relationship between time and distance walked.

   c. the distance walked, in miles, per minute

   d. the distance walked, in miles, after 0 minutes

2. **a.** Trend lines should represent the relationship between months and cell phone value.

   b. Equations should represent the relationship between months and cell phone value.

   c. the change in the cell phone value per month

   d. the initial cell phone value

3. **a.** $y = 0.5x + 70$

   b. The test score increases by 0.5 points for each additional minute studying.

   c. The test score is 70 after 0 minutes of studying.

4. **a.** $y = -350x + 1,500$

   b. The savings account balance decreases $350 per month.

   c. The initial savings account balance is $1,500.

Day 14 (page 180)

1. Sample answer:

2. Sample answer:

3. Sample answer:

4. Sample answer:

5. Sample answer:

6. Sample answer:

Day 15 (page 181)

1. **a.** 1

   b. 2

   c. $y = x + 2$

2. **a.** −2

   b. 10

   c. $y = -2x + 10$

3. **a.** 1.5

   b. 3

   c. $y = 1.5x + 3$

4. **a.** −150

   b. 500

   c. $y = -150x + 500$

5. **a.** 4

   b. 2

   c. $y = 4x + 2$

6. **a.** −1

   b. 30

   c. $y = -x + 30$

Learn about Variability and Probability (page 182)

Example 2

1. 1, 2, 3, 4, 5, 6

Example 3

2. $\frac{10}{3}$ or $3.\overline{33}$

Day 16 (page 183)

1. **a.** 33
   b. 8.8

2. **a.** 200
   b. $45\frac{3}{7}$

3. **a.** 35.5
   b. 14.125

4. **a.** 400
   b. $130\frac{4}{7}$

5. **a.** 58
   b. 24.2

6. **a.** 429
   b. 111.75

7. **a.** 66
   b. 12

8. **a.** 81
   b. 29.75

9. **a.** 46
   b. 13.5

10. **a.** 186
    b. 55

Day 17 (page 184)

1. heads, tails

2. red, blue, green, yellow

3. blue, blue, blue, blue, red

4. 1H, 1T, 2H, 2T, 3H, 3T, 4H, 4T, 5H, 5T, 6H, 6T

5. HHH, HHT, HTH, HTT, THH, THT, TTH, TTT

6. 1, 2, 3, 4, 5, 6, 7, 8, 9, 10, 11, 12

7. 1, 2, 3, 4, 5, 6, 7, 8, 9, 10

8. Student 1, Student 2, Student 3, Student 4, Student 5, Student 6

9. M, A, T, H

10. 1, 2, 3, 4, 5, 6, 7, 8, 9, 10

Day 18 (page 185)

1. not random

2. random

3. not random

4. random

5. not random

6. random

7. not random

8. random

Answer Key *(cont.)*

Day 19 (page 186)

1. a. $\frac{1}{6}$
   b. $\frac{1}{2}$
   c. $\frac{1}{2}$

2. a. $\frac{1}{8}$
   b. $\frac{1}{2}$
   c. $\frac{1}{4}$

3. a. $\frac{1}{4}$
   b. $\frac{3}{4}$
   c. $\frac{1}{2}$

4. a. $\frac{1}{16}$
   b. $\frac{1}{2}$
   c. $\frac{3}{16}$

5. a. $\frac{1}{2}$
   b. $\frac{2}{3}$
   c. $\frac{1}{2}$

6. a. $\frac{1}{2}$
   b. $\frac{1}{5}$
   c. 0

Day 20 (page 187)

1. 100 times
2. 50 times
3. 75 times
4. 25 times
5. $\frac{1}{4}$
6. 100 times
7. $\frac{1}{13}$
8. 20 times
9. 20 times
10. 100 times

Learn about Two-Way Tables (page 188)

Example 1

1. Steak Row: 60%, 40%, 100%
   Chicken Row: 38%, 62%, 100%
   Total Row: 48%, 52%, 100%

2. Male Column: 56%, 44%, 100%
   Female Column: 34%, 66%, 100%
   Total Column: 45%, 55%, 100%

3. 55.36%

Day 21 (page 189)

1.

	7th Graders	8th Graders
pizza	78	84
hamburger	29	36
salad	8	12
total	115	132

2.

	Girls	Boys
candidate A	14	11
candidate B	6	3
total	20	14

3.

	7th Graders	8th Graders
dog	12	9
cat	9	5
total	21	14

4.

	12-Year-Old Friends	13-Year-Old Friends
rock	12	15
country	9	4
rap	8	3
total	29	22

Day 22 (page 190)

1.

	Boys	Girls	Total
red	11	13	24
blue	19	17	36
total	30	30	60

a. approx. 54.2%
b. $\frac{11}{30}$
c. 50%
d. $63\frac{1}{3}$%

2.

	Male	Female
sent email	15	12
did not send email	3	2
total	18	14

a. $\frac{15}{27} = \frac{5}{9}$
b. 27 emails
c. approx. 14.3%
d. 56.25%

3.

	Yes	No
ages 18–25	60	20
ages 26–40	35	10
ages 41–60	40	55
total	135	85

a. approx. 44.4%
b. approx. 61.4%
c. $\frac{45}{220} = \frac{9}{44}$
d. approx. 22.2%

Day 23 (page 191)

1.

	Teens	Adults	Total
sports drink	72.73%	27.27%	100%
water	40%	60%	100%
total	55.32%	44.68%	100%

2.

	Teens	Adults	Total
sports drink	61.54%	28.57%	46.81%
water	38.46%	71.43%	53.19%
total	100%	100%	100%

3.

	Boys	Girls	Total
buy lunch	66.67%	33.33%	100%
pack lunch	36.36%	63.64%	100%
total	54.76%	45.24%	100%

4.

	Boys	Girls	Total
buy lunch	73.91%	44.74%	60.71%
pack lunch	26.09%	55.26%	39.29%
total	100%	100%	100%

Day 24 (page 192)

1. a. approx. 51.85%
   b. approx. 35.71%
   c. approx. 47.37%
   d. approx. 65.38%

2. a. approx. 40.28%
   b. 57%
   c. approx. 55.47%
   d. 29%

3. a. approx. 55.24%
   b. approx. 27.27%
   c. approx. 68.97%
   d. 36%

4. a. 50%
   b. approx. 15.73%
   c. approx. 12.82%
   d. approx. 20.22%

Day 25 (page 193)

1.

	Have a Part-Time Job	Sports/ Clubs	Band/ Chorus	Total
male	10	75	15	100
female	30	50	65	145
total	40	125	80	245

2.

	Have a Part-Time Job	Sports/ Clubs	Band/ Chorus	Total
male	4.1%	30.6%	6.1%	40.8%
female	12.2%	20.4%	26.5%	59.2%
total	16.3%	51.0%	32.7%	100.0%

3. 75%
4. 75%
5. approx. 44.8%
6. 18.75%

7.

	Walk	Ride Bus	Dropped Off	Total
7th grade	32	30	40	102
8th grade	13	90	10	113
total	45	120	50	215

Answer Key *(cont.)*

8.

	Walk	Ride Bus	Dropped Off	Total
7th grade	14.9%	14.0%	18.6%	47.4%
8th grade	6.0%	41.9%	4.7%	52.6%
total	20.9%	55.8%	23.3%	100.0%

9. approx. 71.1%

10. approx. 29.4%

11. approx. 8.8%

12. 75%

Cumulative Review

Day 1 (page 194)

1. $\frac{92}{99}$
2. $\frac{x^2 y^2}{3}$
3. 3.4
4. 8
5. $-13.9, -13\frac{3}{5}, -13\frac{1}{6}, -\frac{130}{10}$
6. 6 and 7
7. 9
8. $y = 2x$

Day 2 (page 195)

1. 11.4
2. yes
3. a. $\sqrt{67}$
   b. $8\frac{7}{8}$
   c. $\sqrt{95}$
4. no
5. 3.2×10^3
6. 225
7. 25
8. 27°

Day 3 (page 196)

1. Sample answer: 1 and 5
2. Sample answer: 1 and 4
3. 102°
4. 78°
5. Sample answer: 1 and 2
6. 78°
7. supplementary
8. 360°

Day 4 (page 197)

1. a. 0.5
   b. 0
   c. $y = 0.5x$
2. 68°
3. two translations OR reflection and translation OR rotation and translation

4. 628 yd.^{3}

5. no

6. 2×10^2

7. 121

8. $\frac{12}{5}$

Day 5 (page 198)

1. negative association
2. yes
3. $2\frac{4}{9}$
4. yes
5. 14.77056 in.^{3}
6. a. yes
   b. no
7. -24
8. $\frac{18}{6}, 3.1, \sqrt{15}, \sqrt{24}$

Day 6 (page 199)

1. Leo
2. Function A
3. $16x^6$
4. approx. 44.58 m^3
5. no solution
6. $y = \frac{1}{3}x + 8$
7. >
8. $10^2 = 100$

Day 7 (page 200)

1. yes
2. irrational
3. approx. 1,071.79 ft.^{3}
4. a. no
   b. 2
5. $(-2, 3)$

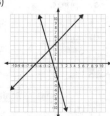

6. $8x^7$
7. yes
8. Function A

Day 8 (page 201)

1. nonlinear
2. 2×10^2
3. no
6.

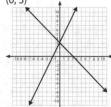

7. yes
8. Function X
4. yes
5. 6,028.8 cm^3

Day 9 (page 202)

1. $y = -\frac{3}{2}x$
2.

$$\overset{\sqrt{79}}{\underset{4 \quad\quad\quad\quad 5}{\longmapsto}}$$

13 – $\sqrt{79}$

3. rotation and translation
4. 3,815.1 in.^{3}
5. infinite solutions
6. no
7. 129°
8. 7

Day 10 (page 203)

1. yes
2. $1
3.

$$\overset{\sqrt{76}\quad\sqrt{88}\quad\sqrt{95}}{\underset{8\ 8.1\ 8.2\ 8.3\ 8.4\ 8.5\ 8.6\ 8.7\ 8.8\ 8.9\ 9\ 9.1\ 9.2\ 9.3\ 9.4\ 9.5\ 9.6\ 9.7\ 9.8\ 9.9\ 10}{\longmapsto}}$$

4. reflection across y-axis
5. 11
6. $5x$
7. 67
8. 7

Day 11 (page 204)

1. Sweaters R Us
2. no
3. irrational
4. $(0, 3)$

5. $y = -10x + 500$
6. 540°
7. 9.4
8. 28,134.4 mm^3

Day 12 (page 205)

1. nonlinear
2.

$$\overset{\sqrt{8}\quad\quad\sqrt{11}\quad\quad\quad\sqrt{17}}{\underset{2.5\quad\quad 3\quad\quad 3.5\quad\quad 4\quad\quad 4.5}{\longmapsto}}$$

3. no
4. 34,464.64 cm^3
5. no solution
6. 154°
7. a. -6
   b. -4 or $(0, -4)$
8. 7.9×10^3

Answer Key (cont.)

Day 13 (page 206)
1. yes
2. −2
3. $\sqrt{340} \approx 18.44$
4.
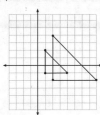

5. a. $-\frac{3}{6} = -\frac{1}{2}$
   b. $-\frac{1}{2}$
6. irrational
7. $x^6 y^{12}$
8. (5, 2)

Day 14 (page 207)
1. a. no
   b. $50
2. no
3. no solution
4. no
5. $y = \frac{3}{2}x - \frac{1}{2}$
6. $y = \frac{10}{3}x + 5$
7. $\sqrt{13} \approx 3.61$
8. −9

Day 15 (page 208)
1. yes
2. yes
3. $y = 8x + 20$
4. 2
5. yes
6. no
7. $g^2 h^2$
8. rational

Day 16 (page 209)
1. a. yes
   b. 30
2. Scenarios should match the graph.
3. no
4. yes
5. no
6. $\sqrt{41} \approx 6.40$
7. 3×10^2
8. a. $x \le 4$
   b.

Day 17 (page 210)
1.
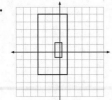
2. $\sqrt{337} \approx 18.36$
3. 4,559.28 in.³
4. linear
5. Graph A
6. no
7. 15
8. $x^6 y^4$

Day 18 (page 211)
1. a. 4
   b. 7 or (0, 7)
2. yes
3. a. 1
   b. 1
4. $\sqrt{505} \approx 22.47$
5. approx. 2,308.39 in.³
6. nonlinear
7. −36
8. yes

Day 19 (page 212)
1. Store B
2. rotation and translation
3. 7
4. $1\frac{2}{9}$
5. $12^2 = 144$
6. −1,748
7. 4
8. 28

Day 20 (page 213)
1. $\sqrt{26} \approx 5.10$
2. 17
3. rational
4. <
5. $\frac{a^2 b^6}{3}$
6. 8
7.

8. yes

Day 21 (page 214)
1. 0.052
2. $\frac{27}{1}$
3. 9 and 10
4.

5. no
6.
7. 105°
8. 180°

Day 22 (page 215)
1. $\frac{27}{100}$
2. 3
3. 5
4. $\sqrt[3]{36}$
5. 70
6. −84
7. $x > 5$

8. x^{12}

Day 23 (page 216)
1. 0.042
2. 2
3. (3, 0)
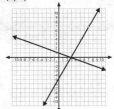
4. 1.092×10^7
5. 8.85×10^3
6. 7,569 m or 7.569×10^3 m
7. 10.3
8.

Day 24 (page 217)
1. $\frac{1}{4}$
2. 23
3. 8
4. 2
5.
6. Company B
7. $9x^6$
8. no

Day 25 (page 218)
1. $\frac{2}{3}$
2. approx. 523.33 in.³
3. irrational
4. 38,750
5. a. 36
   b. 9.6
6. $\frac{1}{2}$
7. 1.39×10^6
8. $\sqrt{37} \approx 6.08$

Digital Resources

Accessing the Digital Resources

The digital resources can be downloaded by following these steps:

1. Go to **www.tcmpub.com/digital**

2. Use the 13-digit ISBN number to redeem the digital resources.

3. Respond to the questions using the book.

4. Follow the prompts on the Content Cloud website to sign in or create a new account.

5. The content redeemed will now be on your My Content screen. Click on the product to look through the digital resources. All resources are available for download. Select files can be previewed, opened, and shared.

For questions and assistance with your ISBN redemption, please contact Shell Education.

       email: customerservice@tcmpub.com

       phone: 800-858-7339

Contents of the Digital Resources

- Standards Correlations
- Class and Individual Analysis Sheets
- Math Learning Resources